Be That Girl

Be That Girl

Ignite Your Passion, Organize Your Life
& Embrace Freedom!

TINA O'CONNOR

Be That Books™

Second Edition

Library and Archives Canada Cataloguing in Publication
O'Connor, Tina
Be that girl : ignite your passion, organize your life & embrace freedom! / Tina O'Connor. — 2nd ed.

Issued also in an electronic format.
ISBN 978-0-9879154-0-5

1. Self-actualization (Psychology). 2. Women—Life skills guides.
3. Women—Conduct of life. I. Title.

BF637.S4O37 2012 158.1082 C2012-902805-3

Text photographs by Tina O'Connor
Cover and text design by Tania Craan
Jacket author photos by Jennifer Herndier, Captured Clix Photography

Published in Canada by Be That Books™
www.bethatbooks.com

ISBN: 0-9879-1540-1
ISBN-13: 978-0-9879154-0-5

Printed and bound in Canada

This book is dedicated to my first coach, Devlyn Steele.

Dev, without your positive influence, I would still be sitting on my butt behind a desk with a snarl on my face. You helped me convince myself that I am amazing, and that happiness was, and always will be, inside of me. You are a compassionate man who is changing the world one protégé at a time with *Tools to Life* (toolstolife.com). I am living proof that you can "fake it 'til you make it" all the way to happiness… and beyond.

Contents

Foreword: *by Robert G. Allen* 11

Introduction: *Be That Girl* 13

Chapter 1: *That Girl Is Me* 15

Meet Tina O'Connor and find out why she was inspired to create the Be That Girl life-changing system.

Chapter 2: *Planet Do It!* 23

Create a Five Year Plan for yourself based on the things you truly want in life.

Chapter 3: *The Home of Your Dreams* 33

Learn about the principles of Feng Shui and how this Chinese method of organizing your home is the key to finding success and fulfillment in the rest of your life.

Chapter 4: *Clearing the Clutter* 39

To organize your home according to the principles of Feng Shui, you must first clear away energy-blocking clutter. This chapter details an efficient action plan to make a de-cluttered home a reality.

Chapter 5: *The Clutter-Free Kitchen* 49

Since the kitchen is the heart of the home, it deserves a chapter unto itself — tips for creating the kind of kitchen that will warm your heart and nourish your soul.

Chapter 6: *Going Green* 59

Getting in the green groove is good for the earth and for you — everything you need to know about recycling and composting so you can Be That GREEN Girl!

Chapter 7: *A Better Arrangement* 71

Re-arrange your home into a sanctuary that will allow you to flourish and make your Five Year Plan a reality.

Chapter 8: *Do It, Do It, Do It!* 87

Don't put off until tomorrow what could be done today — a philosophy that applies as much to tidying up your home as it does to life in general.

Chapter 9: *Time Is on Your Side (Yes It Is!)* 91

Want to reduce stress, increase productivity and find more personal time? These concrete time-management solutions will have you maximizing your efficiency and output in every area of your life.

Chapter 10: *The Infinite Universe* 99

Coincidence? I think not. The Universe is trying to tell you something, so learn how to listen. You don't have to go around the world to figure this out, although if you dream of sunshine and beaches, like Tina does, then you'll be all ears.

Chapter 11: *Accentuate the Positive* 111

Is there a little voice in your head saying you don't have what it takes to Be That Girl? Learn how to kick that voice to the curb and replace it with the voice that says: baby, you got what it takes.

Chapter 12: *Fake It 'Til You Make It* 125

Picture yourself successful. You'll get there by living as if you're there already and by keeping That Girl in mind.

Chapter 13: *Get Dressed For Success* 129

The way you present yourself to the world has a huge impact on how successful you will be — beauty and fashion tips for every girl who wants to believe she's something special.

Chapter 14: *Walk the Walk* 141

To be confident you need to walk confident. Learn yoga-inspired techniques on how to carry yourself and then add your own million-dollar Be That Girl strut.

Chapter 15: *The Power of Touch* 147

Human contact is essential. That includes being comfortable with yourself as a sexual being. Love yourself and you will be able to love your life too.

Chapter 16: *Taking on the World* 153

Being confident in the art of conversation, communication and negotiation is a crucial element of success. Learn more about how to present yourself to the world in a way that is impossible to ignore.

Chapter 17: *Don't Do It Alone* 167

Learn how to ask for help and to love getting it. Aspire to build the right team in every area of your life.

Chapter 18: *Work It Girl!* 175

Are you getting the kind of results you want from your job? Or are you stuck in a daily grind that is wearing you down? Maximize your working life and re-think traditional concepts about employment and retirement.

Chapter 19: *Be Well* 185

If you want to Be That Girl, you've got to be healthy. This chapter has a wealth of useful tips to maintain a healthy weight and eat a healthy diet.

Epilogue 199

Acknowledgements 201

"Tina's book is a delight in so many ways. It offers simple, common sense advice in a direct, no nonsense, non-judgmental style with great use of humor. Thanks, Tina for pointing out the many things which we already know but somehow need to see in writing to hit home."

FOREWORD

by Robert G. Allen

"The future you see is the future you get."
— Robert G. Allen

There are some girls who just have it. There are some girls who want it. Then there are the girls who have it, and can inspire others to get it. Tina O'Connor is That Girl!

In Be That Girl, Tina's driven, energetic personality flows onto the pages, and her encouraging words keep even the skeptics focused. The Be That Girl system features proven strategies that are easy, effective and will give you extraordinary results. Do not settle for ordinary again.

In writing Be That Girl, Tina has proven that the techniques she uses, and teaches, work. From Liquor Store Maven to Successful Author in 1 year…she's proving that it's all in the training. Be That Girl will help you realize that you can be, and do, whatever you want if you are willing to learn.

Be That Girl is a "Happiness System". You will be encouraged to focus on your deepest dreams and goals. You will be given specific exercises that will motivate you and attract everything you need to you. You must be prepared to do the work. It's the 'doing' that will get you results.

You need to commit to the process of you. This is your life, after all, and you are the architect. You need to decide what you are willing to do to get what you want.

You will have to take action. You will have to make decisions. You will create everything you want, and need.

Open yourself up to realizing where you are right now, and allow yourself to be inspired to go wherever you want with Be That Girl.

Start seeing yourself as That Girl today- whoever she is for you. See Her and then Be Her.

Enjoy the journey as Tina walks beside you down a trail of happiness, tidiness, and success.

And don't forget to buy a journal, or two. Your successes will fill volumes.

To Your Success,

Robert G. Allen
Co-Author of *New York Times* Bestseller,
The One Minute Millionaire: The Enlightened Way to Wealth

PS. If you are That Guy, like me, watch for the release of Tina and Ryan O'Connor's book *Be That Guy*, coming soon!

INTRODUCTION

Be That Girl

"Action is the foundational key to all success."
– Pablo Picasso

Be That Girl.

You know exactly the kind of girl I am talking about. Successful, confident, well dressed, happy, healthy, living the life of her dreams. Calm and strong, positive and focused, she always seems to get what she wants and is able to get an amazing amount done in a day.

Who is That Girl? That Girl is you.

No matter who you are, if you are reading this book, you want something different from your life. You want to make changes, be more efficient, less stressed out, more successful, more in control, happier, wealthier, healthier, greener and, well, just more amazing!

Whatever it is that you are looking for, I want to help you achieve it. I want to help you realize you are in full control of your life. I will show you how to attain that control, to take charge of who you are right now and get yourself to where you want to be sooner rather than later.

This is not just another "how-to book," this is a *life changing system*. Throughout this book, you will be given information, but you will also be given a series of action-oriented activities. You will be required to do some work beyond simply reading this book if you want to realize your dreams and create the life you want.

You can have it all. You can have whatever you want. I can give you the tools to make it all possible, but you must be willing to move forward and take action. So be committed. Be ready.

Be That Girl... starting today!

CHAPTER 1

That Girl Is Me

"The possession of anything begins in the mind."
– Bruce Lee

I'd like to believe that my "fiery" temperament has something to do with my being born in the Year of the Dragon. I was truly the kind of child that would not take "no" for an answer and to this day I still have the tendency to kick and scream when I do not get what I want. My husband Ryan has seen temper tantrums that would make a three year olds pale in comparison — we're talking face down on the bed, beating my fists on the mattress and screaming into the pillow out of frustration! Granted, the last time this happened was years ago. I have since learned to deal with my emotions much more maturely. I will be the first to admit that I am not perfect. But I can say with confidence that I am very happy.

I was the first of three children and eagerly took on responsibility without needing much of a push. Even as a kid, I always wanted to be a grown-up. I can remember fantasizing about one day receiving mail addressed to me and thinking about what it would be like when I no longer had someone telling me what to do. Being so independent from a young age caused a lot of headaches for my parents (I love you Mom and Dad; thanks for putting up with me!) and for me as well. I saw asking for help as a major sign of weakness. I have since learned that trying to get everything done on your own is what causes those headaches and that getting the right help and support is a key element if you want to succeed in all aspects of life.

When I was in Grade 3, I distinctly remember a sweet little girl in my class. She was mousy, quiet and shy. She had unflattering glasses and her hair was always a bit messy. She really didn't have any friends. Her external radar was screaming: "Don't look at me, don't talk to me and please leave me alone!" I made a point of being kind to her. I remember thinking to myself that I could help her. I wanted to give her a makeover, teach her how to do her hair nicely, help her be more confident in herself and integrate better with the rest of the class. Didn't she want to be more open, have more connections with people, feel happier about herself and smile more? Maybe she did, maybe she didn't. The point is, I can say that even as far back as Grade 3, I had a keen sense of observation when it came to people and relationships and the desire to help those around me reach their full potential.

My father was an entrepreneur and started his own radio-technology business while he was still in his twenties. As he pursued various business opportunities, our young family moved often, landing in a series of small towns across the provinces of Alberta and British Columbia in Canada. We lived in all manner of trailer parks, apartments and houses, before we settled in the city of Calgary, Alberta, which was the best place for Dad's wireless communication business to flourish. Any kid who moved a lot knows how good it feels to finally stay in one place!

All that moving certainly fueled my outgoing nature. I was motivated to have friends and not be just the strange new girl all the time. When we arrived in Calgary, I was going into Grade 7, the first year of junior high school in Alberta. Even though all the kids were new to the school, on that first day everyone seemed to know each other already. In my first class of the day, I assessed the room and decided which kids looked like good friend material. As for how I would break the ice, I had a secret weapon: colored pens.

BE THAT GIRL

Take Risks! The status quo will get you nowhere. Don't be afraid to do things differently than everybody else.

I walked right over to my potential friends and asked them if they would like to borrow one of my pens. They were receptive to my offer; however, as soon as class ended they just kind of pretended that I did not exist. I refused to give up. I stuck to them like glue for the rest of the day.

They did eventually warm up to me; I think it might have been because I wouldn't leave them alone! In any case, my persistence had gotten me right where I wanted to be... with the "in crowd." Believe me when I tell you that going over to a table full of junior-high kids I did not know gave me an intense feeling of fear in my stomach and made my palms sweat like crazy. To this day, it remains one of the scariest things I have ever done. But I think back to that day often.

Most people are afraid of doing the things that can get them the biggest results in their lives. I believe that experience showed me that when you get beyond your fear and doubt, you are able to achieve the things your heart truly desires.

When I was 13, I decided that I didn't want to have to explain how I was spending my lunch money, so I decided to start earning my own and got myself a part-time job at the Dairy Queen close to our home (I'll bet I can still make the most beautiful DQ soft-serve curl). The owners were very cool guys and, subconsciously, I believe they inspired me to pursue my goal of one day running a business of my own. Everything we do in our lives, every person we meet has an influence on us. We are being given the information we need to succeed every day. We always need to be aware of that and to be listening to what is going on around us.

From that point on, I was never without a job. After Dairy Queen, I became a cashier at Safeway. I still remember the codes for bananas and grapes, 4011 and 4022.

I graduated from high school and attended university where I achieved a Bachelor of Science degree in Psychology and published two academic articles on rat brain surgeries that I performed while working in a neuroscience lab.

After university, I logged seven years doing office and accounting roles at an innovative manufacturing company, before my husband and I took the plunge and started our own business, which I currently run while he holds down a full-time job in the technology industry.

These days, I'm what you'd call a "mompreneur." I own and operate our two successful On The Rocks Liquor Stores, with several more locations planned. As the owner of this little business empire, I only "work" eight hours a week, doing what I choose to do. I have the flexibility to be writing this book and spending time with my three beautiful daughters. For the past three years I have also kept a weekly Wednesday lunch date with my mom and my sister (TGIWWW!). My Uncle Phil has termed this "Wicked Women's Wednesday" based on the fact that there tends to be white wine involved.

I previously mentioned my husband, Ryan, the love of my life. Together with our daughters we live in a home we own in a pleasant acreage community just minutes outside the city. Ryan and I recently fulfilled our dream to travel through Italy on our 10th wedding anniversary. We left the kids at home with grandma and were like teenagers again! He's truly an amazing man.

Looking back, I can easily pinpoint the things in my life that got me to where I am today. My success is tangible and duplicable. In this book, I will share those things with you and help you get what you want out of life also. I have waded through count-

The O'Connor Family. Every family is a gift that should be cherished. Time flies, so enjoy every moment!

less books, listened to tons of advice (good and bad) and gone through years of trial and error.

There have been many mistakes and lots of tears and laughter to get to this point. I want to help you by passing on only those resources that I have found that *actually worked*. I have a true belief and confidence in myself that I can accomplish anything. I want to help instill that same confidence and belief in you, so you can start creating whatever it is you want.

Time always goes by too quickly and it seems there are never enough hours in the day. However, we can always be more efficient — in essence, we can "make" time. If you are able to distill *only the best and most useful things* that you are given each day and apply these things to your life appropriately, it will set you apart from others.

When it comes to getting what you want in all aspects of your life, there is no need to reinvent or come up with a new way of doing things. It's better to borrow the tips and techniques from others that are working for them and that will get you the same results. My brother calls this "poaching and merging," while my kids would call it "copying." (When I hear my kids say: "mom, she's copying me!" I simply tell them that other people will only copy you if they like what you are doing, so it should make you feel excited that they are copying you). I like to call it the "cookie-cutter" approach; it sounds nicer and makes me think of home.

BE THAT GIRL

If you are presented with an opportunity to do something adventurous (like Scuba diving or skydiving) do it! Even if it scares you.

Remember though, that duplicating what others have done can have both positive *and negative* results. People are always willing to give out free advice (which my dad says is "worth exactly what you pay for it"). But be careful. Ask yourself, does the advice really work? Is that person getting the desired results out of what they are doing?

Consider for instance, the process of selecting a financial planner. I always wonder how much money they have made using the same financial advice they are passing on to me.

Are they on track to accomplish their own financial goals? If they have enough knowledge to be making great investments and know what it takes financially to realize their dreams, then why are they still working a nine-to-five office job? In my opinion, the best financial planner is one who is already sitting comfortably on a huge nest egg, has retired early and has chosen to mentor other people to do the same.

These would be the results that I would expect to receive from sound financial-planning advice, so I would seek out someone who had already done it to teach me.

This line of thinking is applicable to anyone from whom you elect to take advice or accept help. The best mentor is one who can provide you with practical advice and proven results. So always be careful when someone gives you advice. Do they have the same values as you? Have they gotten the results that you want? Do they have the education required to intuitively pass on the appropriate information? Though information may be offered to you, it is up to you to decide whether that information is appropriate for your specific needs. Filtering information appropriately generates efficiency and awareness, which leads to success and abundance.

Time is money, and taking the time to read *anything* utilizes valuable resources. I want you, the reader, to know that I care about you and about your time. I want you to know the person you are getting your advice from, so that you can then decide whether the advice that I am offering you is worth your time.

This book is real. It is authentic. It is me. The things I am putting in this book are things that work for me. They are things I have used and things I am actually using right now in my own happy life.

My goal with this book is to give you an actual plan for organizing all aspects of your life. Organization is the key to success, and I will prove it.

You, the reader, will be my amazing success story. If you follow the step-by-step instructions throughout this book, you will feel better about your life, and trust me, things will really start happening for you! The changes you make will make your life better. I have compiled in this one book all of the advice and all of the tools that I have personally been given or used in my life to get me to where I am. Let me be your mentor. I will guide you on your journey to "amazing" and help you find your life balance.

But remember, you are the one doing the work. This is all about you and you are already amazing. My job is to help you convince yourself that you are amazing, and that you can do whatever your heart desires. The rest will all fall into place after that. You were drawn to this book instinctively and I want you to know that you have made the right choice. You are on the right track. The

Universe is smiling on both of us right now because we are about to share such an abundant path together. Thank you for choosing to walk this path with me. I will do everything I can to help you realize your dreams and I trust that you are prepared to do the same. This advice and information will change your life if you are prepared to do the work.

Now, let's get started!

"The Planet Do It portion was the most rewarding and fulfilling hour of my life."

CHAPTER 2

Planet Do It!

"Whatever the mind of man can conceive and believe, it can achieve."
— W. Clement Stone

When I told my husband that I was planning to write a book, he just looked at me and very softly and slowly said: "*Okay*..."

Obviously, he needed some convincing, so I just started talking and talking and before long I had laid out the whole shebang, detailing what this book was going to be about and how excited I was to create it (those who know me well understand that when I get excited, I am usually bouncing-off-the-walls and hard to calm down).

Apparently, I did a decent job explaining my latest crazy idea, because a few days later Ryan came to me and said: "You've got to call one of your chapters, *Planet Do It*."

It's a long-running joke between Ryan and I that we are from "Planet Do It." We have been together 20 years now, long enough to have proven to each other that if you *plan it*, and then *do it*, you can accomplish pretty much anything.

Ryan and I joke that we are from Planet Do-it. Remember, the couple that plays together, stays together!

Last week, at the end of a wonderful family dinner of Chinese food (our favorite!), I cracked open my fortune cookie and read the following words:

"Good luck is the result of great planning"

The Universe was speaking my language! In my opinion, nothing could be more true.

I am sure we have all been guilty of jealously passing judgment on people, saying self-defeating things like: "She is so lucky! She was just born with that body!" When you chalk life up to luck, it is completely out of your control. But when you take luck out of the equation you become responsible for your life. This gives you an amazing amount of power. You now have control. Luck is abstract and spending your days hoping for it will not help you to achieve your dreams, whereas planning will get you to where you want to be.

Sounds simple, right? Sure, but first, you have to get past yourself and that can be the hardest part.

The very first thing you need to do in order to get what you want is to *figure out what you want*! Knowing this is the key. It is time to be honest with yourself. Really, really honest. This is about what you want. Not what your parents want for you, or what your partner wants for you or what your boss wants for you. This is not even about what you think would be sensible or the best way to pay the bills. This is all about your *dreams*. What is it that you long for? What are your aspirations, your goals? What do you feel is missing in your life? What do you want to improve? What would you like to change? You need to be specific here and you need to be personal.

We'll start by breaking things down. Grab some paper — any kind of paper will work for now. I want this to be easy for you and I want you to be able to do it right now. Two sheets of paper should do it. At the end of this book, you will find several blank pieces of paper that you can use for this exercise. No excuses! Do it NOW!

It's important that you don't feel overwhelmed, so let's focus on just six areas in your life.

Copy the following list down, leaving a good amount of space between each item to accommodate more writing.

1. **Relationships**
    a.
    b.
    c.
2. **Travel**
3. **Career**
4. **Money**
5. **Self**
6. **Things**

Now, I'm asking you: What would you like to improve/change/have in those areas of your life? Don't start writing anything yet, just sit and think about that question for a moment. Below are some ideas to provide inspiration. Feel free to use any of the ideas listed here, but be sure to connect to them in a personal way.

1. **Relationships**
    - I want to find a partner who is my best friend and wants to do everything with me.
    - I want to improve my relationship with my parents.
    - I want to have a closer relationship with my children.
    - I want to have children of my own.
    - I want to reconnect with my long-lost best friend, or find a new one.

2. **Travel**
    - I want to travel to anywhere outside the town where I live.
    - I want to travel anywhere outside of the country where I live.
    - I want to travel around the world... I want to go everywhere!
    - I want to go to Las Vegas for the weekend.
    - I want to live in Italy.
    - I want to walk into the airport in the middle of the day with no luggage and get on the next flight out to wherever I want, and then buy everything I need when I get there!

3. **Career/Education**
    - I want to quit my crummy job. I am so unhappy.
    - I want a promotion within my company.
    - I want to find a job that pays me (insert amount) per year/hour/month.
    - I want to work for a boss or an organization that appreciates and respects the job I do.
    - I want to start my own business. (If you know what type of

business you want, such as a floral shop, write that down, otherwise just leave it open).

- I don't want to work anymore. I want to stay home and raise my children.
- I want to upgrade and get my high-school diploma.
- I want to go back to school and become a (fill in the blank).

4. Money

- I want to make (insert amount) per year in my job.
- I want to get a raise (doesn't matter how much, or else specify a specific amount).
- I want $50,000 to be able to move to Italy.
- I want $100,000 for a shopping spree on Rodeo Drive with my mom and my sister.
- I want $5,000 to take my kids to Disneyland.
- I want to help others by donating a portion of my income and time.

5. Self

- I want to be less stressed, have more fun and be more relaxed.
- I want to lose weight (or gain weight).
- I want to be healthier.
- I want to do more yoga (or hiking, or join a softball team or tennis club).
- I want to go for a pedicure every month and have cute-looking toes all the time.
- I want to play golf Wednesday and Friday mornings before work and Tuesday and Thursday evenings after work.
- I want to read my book for one hour every Sunday.
- I want to hire a housecleaner.

6. Things

- I want a downtown high-rise condo.
- I want a house on an acreage.

- I want an expensive new sports car (or a vintage '68 Ford Mustang).
- I want a pair of Jimmy Choo's... and a pair of Manolo's, and a large, walk-in closet to store them in.
- I want a diamond ring, of the engagement variety, or for no reason at all.
- I want a new set of golf clubs and some cute golf outfits.
- I want a motorbike or a scooter.
- I want a car that's reliable.
- I want a house/condo/apartment that is all MINE!
- I want a new computer.
- I want a dog, or a cat.
- I want it all. I am a woman!

Okay, it's your turn now. Take a second to think about each of those areas in your life — *only a second, though* — and then just let your ideas spill out. Feel free to "poach and merge" anything from my list, just make sure it is really something *you* want. Write as much as you can under each category without passing judgment about whether you can or cannot do these things, or what it would take to do these things. Break down all the walls that you have built up over time about who, or what, you are, and allow yourself to be redefined in your own mind. Make sure you think of *at least one thing* for each category before you move on and don't worry about how many things you have. This is not a contest. The more specific and honest you are, the better off you will be.

Allow yourself to write things down even if you don't have the specifics mapped out in your head just yet. For example, say you want to start your own business, but you do not know what kind of business it would be. Just write down your motivation to start one and we'll work on the rest later. Do not allow yourself to think of why you cannot do these things. For now let's pretend that there is nothing holding you back from what you want to do. Literally, for the time being, consider that you have hit the life jackpot and you can now do anything. Think as if there are no restrictions, no fear and no limitations. The more outrageous that you allow yourself to be with this exercise, the more you are opening yourself up to the infinite possibilities of you. Be ridiculous!

As Dr. Seuss once said:

> "I like nonsense, it wakes up the brain cells. Fantasy is a necessary ingredient in living, it's a way of looking at life through the wrong end of a telescope, which is what I do, and that enables you to laugh at life's realities."

So, here we are. Did you really do this task? Honestly? Did you actually write stuff down? If so, I am proud of you! This is an important step toward wanting to make a change. If not, please consider doing it now. Writing down your heart's desires with your own hand helps reinforce these desires, and gets your subconscious working for you. It will make such a difference in the changes that you experience. I can wait, so go for it. I am so excited for you! Take your time, focus, and allow all your inner desires to surface before your eyes...

How do you feel after writing all those things down? I hope you feel exhilarated.

Now for the real challenge. Read over your list and pick the one thing (only one for now) from each category that excites you the most, the one thing that you *most want* from each category. Again, be honest with yourself. This is about you and no one else. Don't limit yourself, or think about what it would take to possibly accomplish these things. Just choose the thing that feels good way down deep inside. Mark each of those items with a little star.

Now, I want you to start with a clean, fresh, new sheet of paper. Track down one of your favorite pens. Choose one that writes nicely, or is your favorite color. This will be your "good copy," so give it the attention it deserves. At the top of your clean sheet of paper, in the right hand corner, write today's date in small letters. Below that, but still at the top of the page, write the following: "I am so happy and proud of myself that I have, or have accomplished, all of these things."

Next, I want you to transfer the six starred items from your initial worksheet onto the nice clean sheet with the date. You are going to rewrite each item on your list in the present tense, rather than the future tense.

Instead of "I want" or "I wish," write "I have," or "I am doing..." pretend that you already have, or are doing these things *right now*. List your six items in whatever order you like. Now, I want you to read over those six items. Wow! Look at all of your goals and dreams and aspirations! You really are the kind of person that knows what they want in life!

At the top of the page, as your title, I want you to write (insert your name)'s Five Year Plan. At this point, you may choose to be done with your plan. If you want, you can embellish your page with stickers or pictures or drawings— anything that makes it feel special and personal to you. Magazine cutouts also work really well. My own personal favorite embellishments are a happy face and a heart or some balloons (seriously, it's fun and it makes you feel like a kid again). Go all out, or be simple, this is about what you want, so don't worry about what others would or wouldn't do.

Guess what, you just wrote a Five Year Plan! You are amazing!

Keep the original worksheet of your plan as well. The reason that we did not transfer all of the items is to keep things simple and not make this an overwhelming task, but if you feel that you want to add the other items to your official plan right now, then by all means, please do. Just make sure you have at least one thing from each category so you are well balanced in your life goals and then do whatever feels right after that.

You know what you want and how quickly you want it. This plan is not fixed. The only sure thing in this life is change, so expect to make revisions to your plan over time as new things happen. Don't worry! Change is good.

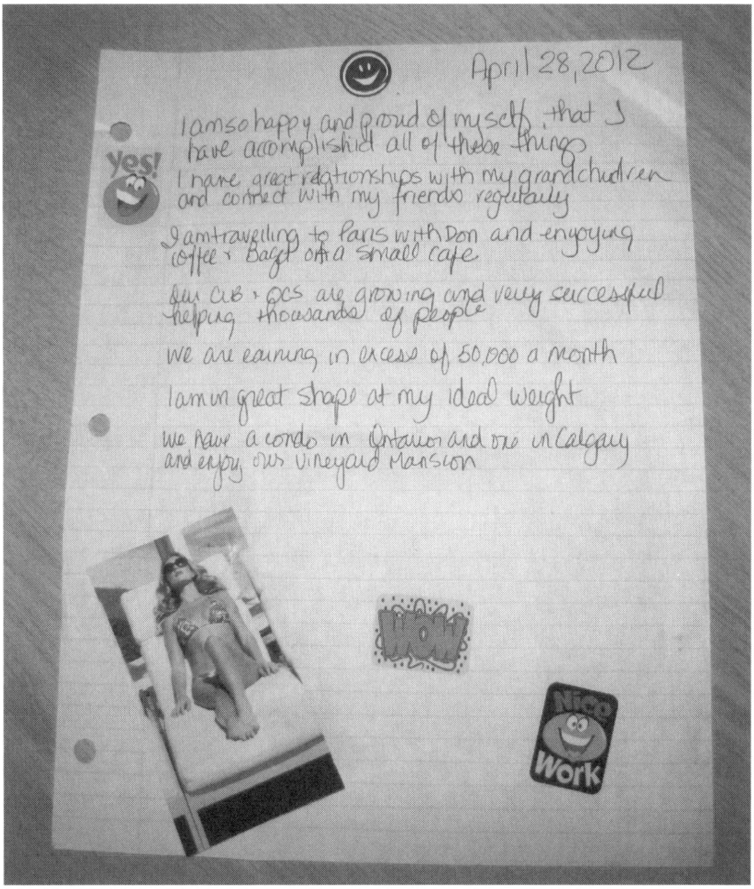

Sample 5 Year Plan. Add pictures, stickers or anything that makes you feel good. Be proud of your plan!

Now, I want you to decide where you will keep your plan in your home. This is a personal choice. If you are a private person, you may choose to fold up your plan and tuck it in your underwear drawer. If you are someone who wants to share her dreams, you might want to pin it up on the wall of your office or beside the calendar in the kitchen. The important thing is that you put it somewhere you won't forget about it. Do what feels right to you. Just seeing your plan often, even if it is folded, will remind your subconscious about your dreams and keep you moving forward.

That's not to say you have to read it over every day — every few months will keep you accountable. When you review your plan, take a good look at the date. Assess where you are in relation to your goals. Make sure you are taking action. You know what you want. Are you on track to get it? Only you will know that for sure.

I know, I know. You have questions. "How will I achieve these goals? I was just writing down a bunch of stuff... I didn't actually think about realizing those goals. It all seems so unrealistic."

Stop that silly self-defeating talk for now and for good. Remember how empowering it felt to write those things down? Let's hang on to that feeling because the rest of this book is going to build on that and help you achieve all those dreams and more. Go and look at your plan posted on the wall, or wherever it is, and think to yourself: "Yes! I have a plan! I have direction. I am on track to get what I want." Just imagine doing, having and improving on all those things from that list. How does that feel? Pretty good, right? Of course it does.

Now that we've figured out where you want to go, let's start working on how we are going to get you there. Have faith in my methods and be prepared to do the work and I will show you how to exact amazing changes in your life. Trust me. I do it every day.

The fastest way to get change happening in your life is to take action immediately. I love to get people going by organizing their surroundings first. Changing things in your surroundings is an action item that produces immediate, tangible results. Taking steps to organize your home will save you time, reduce stress and improve your health, wealth and happiness.

So come with me and let's get organized!

CHAPTER 3

The Home of Your Dreams

"A house is not a home unless it contains food and fire for the mind as well as the body."

– Benjamin Franklin

Now that you know what you'll be working towards for the next five years, it's important that we keep the momentum going and get the right changes in motion.

Let's start at home. Your home is the place to calm your mind and help you focus all your energy in a positive way. Home is where the heart is. It is the place happy memories are made, where your cozy bed and your favorite pillow are. Your home is a shelter that protects you from the elements. It is your space. At the end of a rewarding or exhausting day at work, your home welcomes you into its warm embrace and helps you to relax and put the events of the day aside. At least, this is the way a home should be.

Your home can also protect you emotionally, and physically, and can even help you achieve everything you want in your life. But the other side of this is that your home and the space that you live in can be affecting you in negative ways. There are things you can do to your home that will have positive effects on your life and these things are not overwhelming or difficult. It is easy to take action and see results and I am going to show you how.

First, it's important to understand a bit about the Chinese philosophy of Feng Shui. I was introduced to Feng Shui (pronounced *fung schway*) by one of my dearest friends, Sarah, who I have known since kindergarten. Personality-wise, we are quite different, but we complement each other perfectly. Just as Sarah has shared her knowledge of Feng Shui with me, I'm now going to share my knowledge of this "ancient Chinese secret" with you.

You know how sometimes a room just feels so comfortable that you are compelled to sit down on the comfy couch or chair and just gaze at all the inspiring or interesting things around you? Those rooms where you just feel at peace and present in the moment? On the other hand, I am sure that you have experienced rooms where you did not feel comfortable at all. Even though you might have reluctantly sat down, you likely could not even focus on the conversations taking place because you were preoccupied with thinking about leaving.

Now consider how you feel when you are arranging a room and trying to decide where to position the various furniture items and other features. Do you ever just get a "feeling" about where something should go, though you cannot put your finger on exactly why you feel that way? Essentially, that's Feng Shui at work. The feelings I've just described are evoked by the way the energy moves around in spaces.

There is energy (life force or *chi*) flowing around us at all times. This energy can be good or bad. The goal of Feng Shui is to encourage the flow of positive life energy around you in every room of your home. When positive energy flows around you, then you will be healthier, more at peace and more successful.

Oh yeah! That's what I'm talking about!

Feng Shui is an intricate philosophy and can be considered with varying degrees of complexity. Those of you who are avid scholars will want to delve deep into the background and techniques of Feng Shui. From my own experience I can confirm there to be an overwhelming amount of information out there on Feng Shui and as a researcher you will be bombarded with information — some of it conflicting. Having done my due diligence with both book-based research and real-world experience, I am going to pass on to you a selection of Feng Shui techniques that I have put into use and have found to get results.

Feng Shui is based around a grid called the *Bagua* (see grid below), which is used as a decorating and item-placement guide for your entire home or for individual rooms or areas. As you can see here, the Bagua is separated into sections that correlate to things we are trying to attract in our lives, like wealth, health and love. Each section of the grid has an element associated with it, as well as a specific color. Correctly mapping out your home and identifying each quadrant within your own home is the first step toward applying Feng Shui on a personal level.

Bagua Grid

Wealth and Prosperity Wood Blue, Purple and Red	**Fame and Reputation** Fire Red	**Love and Relationships** Earth Pink, White and Red
Family Wood Blue and Green	**Health and Well-Being** Earth Yellow	**Creativity and Children** Metal White
Knowledge and Wisdom Earth Black, Blue and Green	**Career** Water Black	**Helpful People and Travel** Metal White, Grey and Black

becauseilive.hubpages.com/hub/FengShuiBagua

You will need a blank piece of paper for this home-mapping exercise. To make things more efficient, I have a personal Bagua worksheet available for download on the book's website, www.bethatgirlnow.com.

If you are using a blank piece of paper, draw out a sample Bagua with just the titles of the centers on it, as illustrated on the grid below:

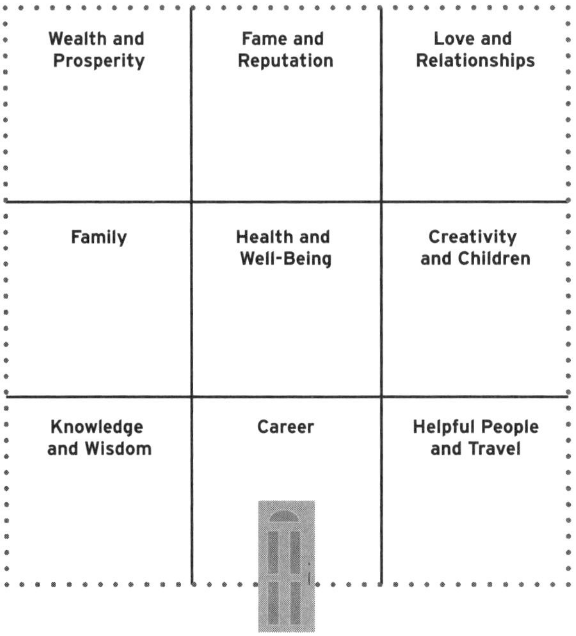

The front door to your home will open into one of the centers along the bottom row: **Knowledge and Wisdom, Career** or **Helpful People and Travel**. If your front door is located directly in the middle of your home, the door will open into the **Career** center. If your door is located more to the left of your home, then it opens into the **Knowledge and Wisdom** center. Similarly, if the door is located more to the right side of your home, then your door will open into the **Helpful People and Travel** center.

Mark the location of your front door on your Bagua worksheet. Now, imagine that you are standing at your front door and looking into your home and start mapping out the rest of the rooms in your home and marking them on the worksheet or paper. (See below for a completed sample).

From the main front door, the room in the furthest left corner will be in your **Wealth and Prosperity** center. Similarly, the furthest right corner of your home from the main entrance door will be your **Love and Relationship** center. I know you can figure out the rest yourself. Add each room to your worksheet.

Wealth and Prosperity Kitchen	**Fame and Reputation** Dining Room	**Love and Relationships** Bathroom
Family Sitting area with Fireplace	**Health and Well-Being** Stairs	**Creativity and Children** Bedroom
Knowledge and Wisdom Dining Room	**Career** Living Room	**Helpful People and Travel** Office

There you go! You have just performed your first Feng Shui mapping exercise.

We are using the main level of your home as a starting point, but once you understand how to use the Bagua, it can then be applied to other levels of your home, as well as each individual room, and even to smaller spaces, such as a desk area.

If you want to apply Feng Shui to your bedroom, for example, stand at the door looking inward. Using the Bagua grid, figure out where the door opens in relation to the whole room (left, right or center). The corner farthest left from the door is the wealth center in your bedroom and so on, according to the grid. The Bagua grid can similarly be applied to your desk area. When sitting at your desk, the corner to the far left is your wealth center.

Now let's pump things up a bit and see how this all applies to your Five Year Plan.

Everything outlined in your Five Year Plan can be related to one of the areas on the Bagua, which, in turn, relates to a specific area in your home. By actively increasing the energy in those centers you will be closer to realizing your dreams in all of those areas. See where I'm going with this?

The Bagua grid specifies certain colors or elements for each center (wealth and prosperity, for example, is represented by blue, purple and red, and by the element wood). You can "pump up" the positive energy in each center of the Bagua by displaying items with the corresponding colors or elements in these spaces. Take, for example, the wealth center: placing a red, wooden object in this area can increase the good energy here. This can be as simple as a plant in a red pot. That said, it is just as important to choose items that appeal to you personally. An item that is wooden and red that you find ugly will not help you. Always respect your taste.

Boosting the good energy levels in the appropriate centers will encourage positive things to happen for you in those respective areas of your life.

By rearranging your home according to basic Feng Shui principles, you will significantly improve your life and realize *all* of your goals. After 15 years of actively applying Feng Shui in my own life, I am still amazed at what can be accomplished just by taking the time every so often to refocus on these principles. Furniture, plant, mirror and fountain placement can greatly improve (or negatively affect) your health, wealth and happiness.

It's time to roll up your sleeves and make your home into the center of success and fulfillment that you deserve.

CHAPTER 4

Clearing the Clutter

"We live within two environments: one is physical and surrounds us; the other is mental and is inside of us. Both can be designed to support your success."
— Darren L. Johnson

Your home is a reflection of you and your family to the world. Are you proud of your home? Do you often have trouble finding things? Do you feel that your home is just too small for all of your stuff? When someone is coming over for dinner, how long does it take you to get your home ready? One hour? Two days? Three weeks?

If there's one thing I've learned from Feng Shui it's this: clutter is bad.

Clutter clouds your mind and reduces positive energy flow in your home. Depending on where your clutter is on the Bagua grid, it will have a direct and significant impact on that area of your life. For example, if there is clutter in your wealth center it will have an impact on your cash flow and wealth generation ability. The good news is that the simple act of clearing the clutter can significantly improve your wealth and prosperity! Dealing with clutter is the most important, and probably the easiest thing you can do, and you *will* see immediate results.

As everyone knows, clutter often piles up following a move to a new home. After our move to the acreage, my office attracted piles of random items: fabric, craft supplies, sewing materials, unfinished projects and various other items.

One Sunday I took it upon myself to get rid of the clutter and hang a picture of mountains behind my desk. The following Tuesday, the bank called to say they would finance a business initiative my husband and I had been pursuing. In addition to that, I ended up selling eight bags of a special weight-loss product that I distribute. On Thursday, I received word that a business project I had been working on was going forward. What a week!

But don't just take my word for it. Take action throughout your own home and you can be the judge of whether it works or not.

I am not asking you to do all of these things at once, but if you do a little in each area, it will inspire you to do more. I guarantee you will like how your space feels when it is neat, tidy and organized. Eventually, you will become an organizing maniac like me and your home will be in pristine condition, ready to welcome company at a moment's notice. You will know where everything is in your home. It will be easier to maintain your organized and decluttered home. Your stress levels will decrease. You will feel happier coming into your "sanctuary" and your life will change forever.

Containing and controlling clutter is a process. Don't bite off more than you can chew, just bite off small pieces. Eventually, you will have eaten the world! Remember that clutter is an ongoing evil, so take steps to manage it everyday.

My first rule is that everything in your home should have a place. If the things you own have a designated space in your home, the items can be found quickly and easily and can be put back where they belong just as quickly, by anyone (even the littlest members of the family).

If you do not have a space for something, do one of two things:

1. Get rid of the item. Throw it out or donate it as quickly as possible.
2. Get rid of something else in order to make room for the item you want to keep.

Be ruthless in determining which things you really need. If you do not have space for something, you must find one or out it goes! Moving to a larger home to accommodate all of your things should not be the goal. Working with the space you have and making things better is the real prize.

The best part about getting rid of things is that the process immediately allows for an abundance of new energy to flow into your life.

Out with the old and in with the new!

Less really is more. As a society, we tend to obsess over and strive for more and more physical things. We tend to value and judge ourselves (and others) by how many things we have, and we believe we earn status through these things as well. We collect various items for many different reasons and then have problems letting these items go because we feel that collecting them makes us who we are and letting go of them will change us somehow. Most people fear change in one way or another, but I urge you to embrace your fears. If you are not where you want to be in your life right now, something needs to change.

Albert Einstein said it best:

"The definition of insanity is doing the same things and expecting different results."

You have the power to create change and it can start ever so simply with the act of clearing out your home.

Start wherever you feel like starting and do as much as you can at the time, but don't ever stop. You need to drill it into your head that this is the most important thing you can do to achieve results in your life. This is an ongoing process and it will always require action. At first it may seem like an impossible and never-ending task, but eventually you will feel like a goddess in a palace. Once that happens, reorganizing and de-cluttering areas of your home will become a one-hour project here and there, whenever it happens to fit your schedule. Your home will continue to get better and more efficient and you will start to see results in every other aspect of your life. But you have to take that first step. So let's get to work.

The biggest piece of advice I have in regards to organizing your home is: DO IT NOW! If you see an area that bothers you, or a pile of stuff on the floor, don't just walk away from it and think: "I'll get to that later." That is how you ended up with clutter in the first place. Being That Girl requires you to be proactive and take action whenever you can. Pick that stuff up off the floor and put it where it belongs immediately. Once you do, you will be able to breathe easier and relax more. More positive *chi* will flow into your life and you will see consistent improvements.

Time to sort!

Choose a manageable area to start. Looking at your Bagua worksheet will help you prioritize your clutter-clearing process.

If you are in need of extra cash, or concerned with your finances in general, start in your wealth corner. If you hate your job, or have been considering a career change, start in your career corner.

If there are areas in your home that have just been driving you crazy, start there! Clear your clutter and you will clear your mind. Eventually you will become so smitten with your tidy, neat space that any area of clutter will drive you mad. You'll get there eventually, but for now, start small.

At this point, I would also like to make a distinction between "neat" and "clean." As you aspire to Be That Girl, understand That Girl also needs to have fun! In this sense, I am not advising you to be Cinderella and spend all your time scrubbing and cleaning (getting what you want might mean hiring a house cleaner). The great thing about getting your home organized and tidy is that no one will notice that it is not 100 percent spotless. The perception will always be that your home is clean, even if it has been a couple of weeks since you scrubbed the place.

Okay, back to sorting. Stuff, stuff and more stuff. Where should it go? Not out in the open on shelves. Not on the floor, and not jammed into already overflowing cupboards. It is useful to have a few black garbage bags, empty boxes, recycling containers or laundry baskets on hand to use for sorting. If you are cleaning a closet, pull absolutely everything out. I did this recently with my craft/recycling cupboard, and I timed the entire project. It took me 40 minutes, start to finish, and the results were amazing. Check out some pictures of my closet reorganization in the following pages.

Do the same with every space in your home. Every item in the room or area must now be assessed and sorted using the following rules:

Keep It!

Things that fall into this category will be one pile. If the item goes in the room you are working on, find a space for it right away — not shoved in a cluttered closet, but somewhere that it is easy to find, access and put away. Otherwise, leave it in the pile with the intention of finding a spot elsewhere. Once you are done clearing the space you are working on, you will put the items from this pile away in their new places. This will also help you determine which area will be your next project.

It never takes long for a cupboard to get to this point, especially when you have kids.

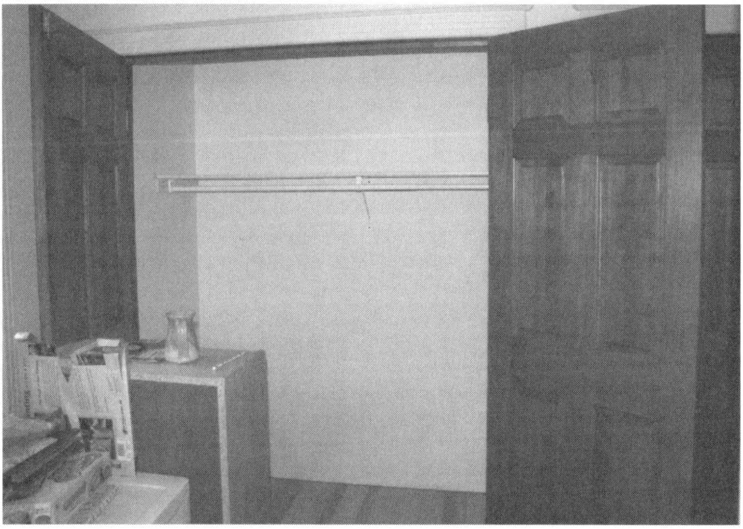

When I say take everything out, I mean EVERYTHING!

Ahhh! Now that is a functional, organized cupboard. I even added stuff to this cupboard! Elapsed time: 40 minutes.

Trash It!

This has become one of my favorite things to do. I am ruthless! If something is broken and not usable or able to be repaired, it needs to go in the garbage. Be honest... are you really going to mend those pants, or glue that Christmas ornament back together? Toss it and feel good about it. Unfinished projects get in the way of good energy. Trash it and move on!

Donate It!

This is the give-away pile. I love donating stuff I don't need if someone out there can use it. This pile is for things that are still usable, but no longer have a place in your life. We have a clothes donation box close to our home that I frequent. It is so easy to do and doesn't take that long. I also love donating to Goodwill. Donating allows you to help others and when you come home to your organized space, you feel amazing too. It's a win-win situation!

Return It!

If part of your clutter involves someone else's stuff that you have borrowed, or stuff that has ended up in your home somehow, put it all in a pile and then make time to return it to the rightful owners as soon as possible.

Sell It!

Taking your usable items to a second-hand or consignment store opens up the possibility of earning money out of your unwanted treasures. You can also use an online classified ad service like *Kijiji* to market used items. Include pictures of your items when you put them online — after all, a picture is worth a thousand words. You can also plan to have a garage sale if you clean out every room in your house. This way, you can make some decent cash with the added bonus of having someone take your stuff away for you. Price your items fairly if you want them to sell, or you will just end up having to donate them. (I hate going to garage sales where people price their stuff really high and then won't budge on the price. Come on, people! You don't want the stuff anymore, right?) Allow yourself to let go of the emotional ties you have to your items and enjoy the fact that someone else is willingly carting them away.

Once you have all your stuff sorted and have put away the items that belong in that particular room, take the other piles out of that area. The stuff that you want to keep will now need to be given space in a different room. Put this pile somewhere like the kitchen, or another high-traffic area, where you will have no choice but to deal with it. Clear away the trash piles and the recycling to the garage, or the bin in the alley.

If you will be dealing with the trash and donated items yourself, load them into your vehicle right away to make it easy for you to deal with on your next trip out. This action also removes the clutter instantly from your home. If there are things that need to be returned to others, put that pile somewhere like the garage where you will see it, then make a point of setting up a time when the owner can drop by or you can visit them to return their items. You may even want to just load these items in the vehicle so that you can easily deliver them on your way home from work.

Either way, the goal is to sort the clutter and then deal with it right away. I promise you will be inspired by the feeling of ultimate satisfaction that comes from seeing these unwanted items reach the trash, recycling depot, second-hand store, donation box or rightful owners. Enjoy that feeling!

Now that the clutter is removed from the room, I want you to take a look around and decide if everything is where you would like it. Take this opportunity to move furniture around, move pictures and other artwork, and generally make the room more appealing and functional. In Chapter 7: A Better Arrangement, I am going to give you tips on furniture placement for every room in the home, but remember, if it feels good to you, that means it is probably great Feng Shui, so listen to yourself. You have all the answers inside you. Take the time to listen.

Savor the results. Revel in the calmness and tranquility that comes from a tidy space and open yourself to the new opportunities that you have just created. Congratulations! You have just achieved one of the most important skills for moving your life forward in a positive direction.

"Last night, I was reading your book, while relaxing in the bath. I am trying to break a really bad habit of falling asleep on the couch, and decided that maybe I would enjoy going to bed more if my room was more inviting. I don't often make the bed, and there are clothes strewn over a chair (rather than in the closet where they belong!). I figured that I should tidy things up, and as I was putting away a sweater, I checked the pocket and found $5. What a nice little surprise reward for putting in the effort to clean up and be organized!"

CHAPTER 5

The Clutter-Free Kitchen

"The best time for planning a book is while you're doing the dishes."
– Agatha Christie

The kitchen is truly the heart of any home, which is why it deserves its own special chapter. Here, the family members gather to nourish themselves at the beginning of the day and at the end of the day. It is here that you prepare healthy foods to nurture your body while the healthy conversation and interaction with your family nurtures your soul.

The kitchen should always be ready to go. You should wake up in the morning to a clean space that is ready for you to prepare the most important meal of the day, breakfast. Counters should be kept clean and clear of clutter (as much as possible). Anything that is not required to be out on the counter should be put away in a cupboard. Remember that clutter will negatively affect your life, and removing it will give you a nice clean slate. I agree that

Imagine waking up to this kitchen in the morning. It's a mess before you even get started! This mess may discourage you from wanting to make a nice, healthy breakfast.

A beautiful, clean kitchen will encourage you to create healthy meals and snacks for yourself and your family. Knowing that your kitchen is clean will subconsciously give you a calm feeling while you are en route to home to prepare the evening meal. Start fresh with each meal by leaving your kitchen in a ready position.

the coffee pot should be on the counter if you use it frequently, so long as it is out of the way of your working space. If you find that you are already cramped as far as counter space, put away the coffee maker, the toaster, the utensil organizer and the canisters and pull out only as needed. If you own a large stockpot that is absolutely necessary for preparing family meals, try to find a spot for it instead of always leaving it out on the kitchen stove.

Can't find space in the cupboards? Get rid of something you don't need. Keep only those things that you use and that enhance your life. Sell or donate appliances and gadgets that you don't use. If you do not care about the money, it will make you feel good to think about the people you will help by donating these items to charity.

While you are clearing the clutter off your counter tops, you will inevitably discover that you need to rearrange your cupboards in order to make room for items you want to keep. Find some time to pull everything out so you can decide what needs to stay and what needs to go. If you haven't used a kitchen gadget in three, six, or twelve months (the appropriate time limit is your call) you probably can make do without it. Take, for example, that juicer your mother-in-law gave you for Christmas three years ago — you know, the one you used a few times during that first month and then abandoned to the back of the cupboard. Use the same "clutter-clearing" guidelines in the kitchen that were outlined back in Chapter 4: Clearing The Clutter.

Time to start sorting. Group items together in a way that makes sense: all of the pots and pans should go together, as should the baking trays, cake pans and muffin tins. Nest all your mixing bowls together and ensure that the items that you use most often are easiest to get to. Keep your reusable leftover containers together. The reusable container drawer can be tough to organize. Here's my tried and true method: stack the round containers together and stack all of the square and rectangular containers inside each other. Use one empty container to store all of the small lids, then

organize the large lids together in a row and secure them using one of the containers as a "book end," as you would on a bookshelf.

You can also use a pot lid-holder to store your reusable lids, as I do with my glass container lids. Only hold on to reusable containers that have a matching lid. This will put an end to the frustration of putting your leftovers in a container and then not being able to find the right topper!

Now, let's take on the pantry. Take everything out and throw away any items that are expired, no longer fresh or that you just will never use. If there are perfectly good, non-perishable items that you or your family do not like, then donate them to the food bank or place them in the food hamper collection bins at your local grocery store. By doing this, you'll make room for new, fresh items. Be brutally honest here. All those exotic sauces that sounded so good in the store but you've maybe used once? Toss them. If, by chance you decide to make that recipe again a year or two down the road, you always have the option of just picking up some more at that time.

You may be surprised at what you find in your pantry. Let's make it so that you are not so surprised from this point forward. Organizing this space will encourage you to use what you have in the house, which will allow you to save money on groceries. I frequently find boxes of goldfish crackers and cheerios with two or three left at the bottom, or a box of granola bars that is completely empty in my pantry. If I see the box in the cupboard, I am not going to put that item on the grocery list, which means that we won't have any granola bars that week.

Let your family know that if the empty box stays in the pantry, that item will not be purchased, or go one step further and put up a whiteboard, chalkboard, or piece of paper somewhere in the kitchen, to function as an ongoing grocery list. Explain to your family that if they see an empty (or almost empty) box, or if they use up the last of something (especially items like sugar and baking powder), the first thing they should do is write that item on the grocery list. The second thing is to get it out of the pantry and recycle the packaging. All it takes is a couple of times of not buying your children's (or husband's) favorite items to ensure that your grocery/pantry rules are followed. Consequences enforce behavior!

Here are my guidelines for organizing the pantry.

The following items should be grouped together:

- Baking-related items
  - Flour
  - Sugar
  - Baking powder/soda
  - Cornmeal, bran, etc.
  - Muffin tins, cake decorations, nuts, food coloring (I have a Tupperware container that I use to store all of these little items in, then I know where they are when I need them, which is not all that often!)
- Rice, pasta and beans
- Sauces, oils and vinegars
- Spices
- Condiments
- Cookies, crackers, snacks and granola bars
- Cereals and oatmeal
- Cans of soup, vegetables and fruit

I use Tupperware products to organize my pantry and I always will. I know that there are arguments against using plastic containers to store food, but pantry items do not need to be frozen or microwaved, so I have decided to continue using them. All of my dry ingredients are stored in labeled containers that stack easily. These containers keep my ingredients as fresh as possible — no bugs or rodents could ever get into my Tupperware! This system is ideal for any climate and if you're someone who frequently leaves your home for extended periods, you'll have the peace of mind that comes from knowing that your food will stay fresh.

When people look at my pantry the most common response is: "You are *soooo* organized!" I have to say that it's the Tupperware that makes me look good! I sold Tupperware for a period of time

An organized pantry should be both efficient and easy to maintain. When everything has a place, things are easy to find and easy to put back. Increase your free time through organization.

so that I could outfit my pantry affordably. I love a good deal and I have always been frugal with my money and I have to say that Tupperware has been worth every penny. Their pantry product line is guaranteed for life and, if you are lucky, sometimes you can find a Tupperware consultant who will come and evaluate your pantry at no extra cost. These consultants will look through your whole pantry and then tell you what you need and how much it will cost. Once all of your Tupperware arrives, the consultant may even help you get everything into the containers for no extra charge. Although, even if you do things yourself, the setup is pretty easy.

BE THAT GIRL

Indulge yourself with luxury grocery items every now and then. A good block of cheese is always a tasty treat. Mmmm... brie....

All right, that was my little love letter to Tupperware and what it can do for your pantry. Now, let's move on to the refrigerator.

Just like you did with the pantry, pull everything out and put it on the counters and on the floor. Take this opportunity to clean the inside of your fridge with a warm soapy cloth. Throw out any fruits and vegetables that look like wrinkly old men. Clean out your vegetable trays. Throw out any leftovers that have been in there for too long (you can be the one to determine that, however, if you don't know how long it has been there, or what it is, that's a pretty good sign that it should be tossed).

Make it a rule to clean out your fridge once a week. I tend to do this when I get back with my groceries, or the night before grocery day. That way the fridge is nice and clean and ready for the new food. You may choose to do this on Sunday night when you are making lunches for Monday morning, or any other day that makes sense for you. When you do this consistently, you will feel so good about your fridge. You will know exactly what's in there, and more importantly, what isn't in there, which helps when you're making your grocery list. Check all the expiry dates on your sauces, salad dressings and condiments and throw out any that are past the date, as well as bottles and jars that are almost empty. Also, dispose of anything that you or your family will no longer eat, even if it is still within the expiry date. No sense keeping it at that point; it's just more clutter in your kitchen.

Once you are satisfied with what you've decided to keep, take this opportunity to rearrange the shelves in your fridge to better suit where you want things. If you have always wanted to be able to store milk and juice on the shelves instead of inside the door, move the shelves around so these items will fit easily. Organize things to your liking, then enjoy the feeling you get when you open your fridge and are able to see everything and know exactly what is in there. It will make putting away your groceries less stressful and, if done consistently, will take very little time. I timed myself once at someone else's house (my desire to organize isn't just limited to my own fridge) and it was a 20-minute project from start to finish. I know most of us can find 20 minutes during the course of an entire week!

Do the same thing with the freezer section of your fridge as well as your deep freeze. Take everything out, determine what is worth keeping, clean with a cloth and then return and organize the items that you are not throwing away. Ridding yourself of unwanted items and knowing that things are clean will give you a feeling of calm at the subconscious level.

Ensure that your kitchen garbage is concealed in a cupboard or closet and not just sitting out somewhere. If the garbage must be out, contain it in a nice-looking garbage bin with a lid. The garbage does need to be accessible so make sure you put it somewhere that is convenient when you are working in the kitchen. Garbage attracts a lot of bad energy, so keep the bad energy levels to a minimum by emptying the garbage as soon as it is full and making sure that the garbage can and its lid are clean, both inside and out. This will make you feel happy about your garbage (imagine that!), keep the smell down and help you create more positive energy in your home.

Before I let you out of the kitchen, here are a few more tried-and-true tips I've learned over the years:

> **Kitchen Tip 1:** Never wash your fruits and vegetables when you get them. Always wash them just before you are going to use them. Washing them right away and then storing them will make them go bad much sooner because of the added moisture.

Kitchen Tip 2: Filling up a sink with cold water and adding some lemon juice is the best and safest way to wash your vegetables and fruits and an effective way to clean your produce of pesticides and bacteria. Immerse your produce for a few minutes and you'll be good to go.

Kitchen Tip 3: According to my BFF Annie, rubbing your cutting board with fresh lemon after cutting meat on it is an effective and natural method of killing germs.

Kitchen Tip 4: To get rid of the smell of onions and garlic on your hands, rub them on the bottom of a stainless steel sink with a bit of water in it. It really works....try it!

Kitchen Tip 5: When boiling pasta, if you place a wooden spoon across the top of the pot, it will stop the starchy foam from boiling over! Thanks for this tip Mom!

CHAPTER 6

Going Green

"Forget not that the earth delights to feel your bare feet and the winds long to play with your hair."
– Khalil Gibran

Living in North America can be like living in a bubble sometimes, especially if you have never experienced life in a third world country. I recently traveled to Central America and had a wonderful time. It was very disturbing to me, however, to see how the native residents of that country dealt with their garbage: burying disposable diapers in the sand on the beach, throwing garbage into the ocean and burning everything, including plastics and aluminum. There were no recycling depots, at least that I could see, and tin cans and bottles were simply tossed in with the rest of the trash. Survival was first and foremost on people's minds and taking care of the earth was not even a thought, let alone a priority.

But really, who can blame them? Most, if they are lucky, will only obtain a Grade 6-level education, after which they are expected to get out and earn a living to help support their families. Feeding themselves and their children is clearly more important than worrying about where their garbage ends up. The experience reinforced my view that those who are fortunate to not have to worry about where their next meal is coming from, who have been educated, and who have the resources to make a difference, need to take the lead on changing the world for the better.

I believe that we all have a social and environmental responsibility to ask ourselves if what we are putting into the garbage is actual garbage. I do hope that you are the "recycling type," and if you are not, I want to teach you to Be That GREEN Girl!

Do you at least recycle your empty bottles and beverage cans? There is almost always a deposit on these items that will be given back to you when they are returned to a depot. Returning empties is one way to save up money that can be put towards realizing one of your goals. My husband and I have been saving our bottle money for a hot tub. It is amazing how it adds up if you set it aside as soon as you get it — put the money in a drawer or in a separate bank account that earns interest and watch the balance grow.

Even when you are away from home or travelling, try to ensure that cans and bottles make it to a recycling depot. We all need to do our part to make sure our world does not end up as it's portrayed in the animated sci-fi movie *WALL-E* (one of our family favorites). If you haven't seen it, the basic gist is that it is set in a time when the world has accumulated so much trash that humans actually have to vacate the planet, leaving behind a fleet of (adorable) trash-compacting robots to do the cleanup.

What I'm trying to say is that I want you to recycle, starting immediately! Do you have a recycling pick-up service where you live for your cardboard and plastics? Some places are fortunate enough to have these items picked up along with their garbage. If you do not have recycling pick-up, consider signing up with an independent company that provides this service on a weekly basis. Typically, these companies charge a small fee (maybe $20 per month) to come and take away your recycling every week. In my mind, this is a small price to pay to know that you are doing your part for the environment. If the $20 a month is too steep, or if this service is not available in your area, find a recycling depot close to your home where you can drop recyclables off yourself.

If there are no recycling facilities in your town or area, consider being the person that inspires your municipal government to install them. Or, start your own recycling pick-up business. Don't just sit around and wait for things to happen… make them happen! This might be a time-consuming process, but in the end it is well worth it. If we all do a little, it accumulates into a huge difference. Conversely, if we all decide to do nothing, or if we think: "What difference can one person possibly make?" then we'll never make any difference at all. By taking charge of the situation yourself, you will be inadvertently affecting others and the more you do, the better you will feel. Be That Green Girl!

So, what can be recycled anyway?

- **Cardboard**

  Cereal and cracker boxes (large boxes sometimes need to be broken down into smaller sections to make them easier to manage). Toilet paper rolls and paper towel rolls (I frequently dig empty toilet paper rolls from the bathroom garbage) and paper towels that have been used only to dry off hands.
- **Plastic Containers**

  Make sure to rinse them out before recycling.
- **Plastic Bags**

  Grocery bags and food bags, cereal bags, Ziploc bags – on this note, I hope that you have thought about, or are already using reusable grocery bags for grocery shopping. I am in the habit of putting my reusable canvas bags in the car when I make my grocery list, which is usually the night before I go for groceries. Most stores are charging for grocery bags now to help eliminate the use of so many plastic bags. If you still use plastic, please consider getting yourself some reusable bags, or make sure that you are recycling or reusing the plastic ones you accumulate.

- **Tin Cans**

  These also need to be rinsed out first.
- **Glass Jars**

  Need to be rinsed.
- **Styrofoam Containers**

  Look for the recyclable symbol on these first, although most are good to go.
- **Paper Of All Kinds**

  Newspaper, coloring books, pretty much any kind of paper around your home.
- **Tetra Paks**

  These can also be returned to depots for a deposit.

I also want to talk a bit about composting. Again, some neighborhoods are lucky enough to have compost picked up weekly as part of their regular garbage service (garbage, recycling and compost pick-up service… if I had this, I would be in heaven!) Even if you do not have compost pickup, consider putting a small composter in your backyard. They do not take up a lot of room, and contrary to what my husband has always believed, they do not smell bad if you are composting properly.

Composting is basically turning natural, organic matter into reusable soil. The process takes "natural" garbage and basically allows it to rot into a dirt-like matter. This matter is rich in nutrients and is amazing for your garden. It is basically a natural fertilizer and it is the earth-friendly way to keep the cycle of life in the garden going. Even if you are not an avid gardener, or if you do not even have a garden, I want you to consider composting. You can always give your compost to that neighbor down the street with the amazing garden, or even sell it.

All you really need to start composting is a square, wooden container with ventilation holes and an open top. You can also purchase plastic compost bins at most hardware/home stores. These bins are reasonably priced and allow you to be up and running immediately. Some cities and towns will even have a day or two each year where they sell composting bins and rain barrels for a fraction of the cost to encourage people to get green.

Composting requires equal amounts of "brown material" and "green material." To start your compost, you will need a layer of "brown material" at the bottom.

"Brown material" consists of:

- Dead leaves, twigs, and branches
- Manure
- Hair and nail clippings

"Green material" consists of:

- Grass clippings
- Fruits and vegetables, including peelings, cores and whole items past their prime
- Eggshells
- Plain rice
- Plain bread
- Paper towels and clean toilet paper
- Coffee grounds
- Beans
- Basically, if it is natural and organic it can go in your compost bin.

What *cannot* go in your compost bin:

- Oils
- Cheese or milk products
- Meat or animal products
- Sauces of any kind

So, just to review: the compost bin is for natural products only. You cannot just dump your leftovers in there. Butter, sauce or oil can't go in. By restricting your compost to organic matter only, and making sure to always add corresponding amounts of brown material, you will not get foul odors. Oils, meat and animal products rotting will attract bugs and animals and will make your compost smell nasty!

Layer the brown and green material, and be sure to turn or mix your compost every few weeks. If it is really dry where you are, you may need to add a bit of water occasionally to help your compost along. Too much water is not good though.

The hotter the weather, the faster you will get nice compost.

If you are an avid gardener, or if you have a large family like me, you will likely need more than one compost bin, and they will all be at various stages. You will end up with glorious garden fertilizer and you will have saved tons of garbage from ending up in the landfills.

Here is a compost pile that I have started in my garden. I ran out of room in my other compost bin, so I started a new pile. I turn it frequently and it is composting nicely. No bin required!

Layering your compost is of utmost importance. Here the layer of brown material is followed by a topping of nice organic green material, some grass clippings, egg shells, potato peels, apple and pear cores, limes, tomatoes, strawberries and some coffee grounds....a typical week of organic waste that will soon be turned into nutrients to feed the garden.

I like to cover up, or finish my compost, with a layer of leaves and dead grasses. This provides a nice layer for me to dump my next week of waste right on top. I then use my empty compost container to collect a bin of brown material for the top. This maintains a healthy balance of brown and green material.

This compost bin has a small door at the bottom that opens up so you can collect your hard earned "compost" to feed your garden. Nice feature!

Here you can see the layers being composted down. At the bottom, the mixture almost resembles dirt. Closer to the top you can still see fragments of egg shells and orange peels. Your compost is ready when you can no longer tell what you originally put into it! It should look like a nice rich soil. What a fantastic way to give our planet back the nutrients that we are taking out of it. Reduce, Reuse, Recycle!

From here on, every time you go to throw something in the garbage bin I want you to ask yourself: "Is this really garbage, or can it be recycled or composted?" The more you do this, the more self-aware and socially conscious you will become. I frequently ask myself questions like: "Should I really be eating this if it cannot be composted?" "Is there a product I can buy that has less packaging?" "Should I be using cloth diapers instead of throwing out all of these disposables?" When you start taking a vested interest and questioning the way things have always been done, you'll soon realize that you *do* have control and that you *can* make a difference. If you weren't a "Green Girl" before, I will turn you into one yet!

So what is garbage? If you take out all of the recyclable and compost items listed earlier in this chapter, it sure does not leave a whole lot, does it? If you are recycling and composting, you will be amazed at the small amount of garbage that accumulates each week. Here are some things that should be labeled as garbage, however, in these instances, I try to question whether or not these items are truly needed, or if we could replace them with a different alternative in the future:

- **Disposable Diapers**
  Can we switch to reusable cloth diapers, or start training our children earlier?
- **Used Tissues And Paper Towels**
  Ready to bring hankies back? There are a variety of cute, reusable handkerchief options that come in attractive carrying cases. If you're not ready to go that far, eliminate the use of paper towels by using washable cloths.
- **Leftover Food**
  Question what you are eating and whether you are making excessive quantities.
- **Used Food Packages**
  If the packaging is not recyclable, perhaps we shouldn't be eating these foods.
- **Broken Or Damaged Household Items And Toys**

There are other items that should not end up in the regular household trash — batteries and empty paint cans for example. There is a special place at your local dump or landfill where these items can be disposed. The same goes for electronics — these also cannot end up in the trash. A lot of businesses take back used electronics for recycling. Do an online search to find out where you can drop off used electronics in your area so they don't end up in the landfill.

Based on all of the above information, you might need to make a few changes in your kitchen in order to accommodate your new "garbage" methods. You certainly won't need that huge trash can anymore, especially since you will be changing out your garbage more frequently and making an effort to reduce, reuse and recycle.

Find a spot in or near your kitchen, preferably a cupboard, closet or pantry, where you can set up a recycling station. I have seen some people who have done this on their back deck or in their garage. The important thing to keep in mind is that your recycling station needs to be accessible in order for it to be effective. The closer the recycling station is to the kitchen (where most of the household waste is produced), the more likely you are to use it. Get a bin or box for cans, bottles and tetra-paks that can be returned to the bottle depot for refund. Make it part of your routine to take these items back before they overrun your home with clutter. Have a second bin or box for other recyclables.

Some recycling depots and pick-up services require you to separate your recycling into plastics, paper, cardboard, etc. If this is the case, you will need a few different bins. Stacking bins are great as they allow you to organize vertically and take up less floor space. Make sure that your bins are easy to access and also easy to remove on recycling-pick-up or recycling-drop-off day. Have a set schedule for when you take care of these items to prevent clutter from accumulating.

As for your compost, keep a small bucket underneath the sink where you can throw your veggie and fruit peelings, coffee grounds, eggshells and other "green material." This organic matter will not smell (unless you put the wrong things in it), so you can set a scheduled time to empty the bucket in the compost bin in the yard.

The size of your family, and how much organic matter you produce together, will determine whether you need to empty your compost bucket daily, every couple of days or weekly. Make sure to throw in a bucket of leaves or other "brown material" when you empty your kitchen compost bucket. Always empty the compost first and throw the brown material on top.

BE THAT GREEN GIRL

If you must use paper towels, buy half-size brands. Consider switching to cloth napkins. Pack lunches with reusable snack containers instead of using plastic wrap or plastic bags.

Being That Green Girl also means being aware of what chemicals you are using in your home, or putting in your body. Here are a few green girl tips.

Green Tip 1: Be cautious of anything that has a strong smell. Most smells are not created naturally, so if something smells strong you can be assured that there are chemicals in it. Most of us have grown up thinking that the strong smell of cleaning products means things are clean and disinfected. In actuality, those strong smells are exposing you and your family to harmful chemicals everyday! Just walking down the laundry and cleaning product aisle in any grocery store can make me feel sick. The smell test applies to everything, including cleaning and laundry products, perfumes, hair care and body care products (such as soap, cream, shampoo), candles, and air fresheners. Look at all of the products you currently use and read the ingredients. This is as important as reading your food labels! Eliminate any products from your home that have chemicals in them. Choose natural or green cleaning products. These are better for you and your family, and better for the environment. Natural products will frequently have no smell, or be infused with natural oils. If you want to enhance the smell of your natural products, add a few drops of your favorite essential oils, like peppermint, eucalyptus, or lavender. Essential oils can add a lot of beautiful aroma, naturally. Keep your exposure of chemicals to a minimum by using your nose!

Green Tip 2: Choose organic and "Grown Close to Home" products. Organic farming is better for the environment and for us. Though it is more expensive right now, if we all make the choice to eat organic, the price will come down because more suppliers will produce it as the demand goes up. Organic foods tend to be smaller and packed with more nutrients. Bigger is not always better in this department. Support your local businesses whenever possible. Eating produce and meats farmed close to your home means that it gets to you quicker, ensuring freshness, and less "preservation". Eat fruits and vegetables that are in season. Berries in winter? Consider how that is possible.

Don't listen to Kermit the Frog. It is easy being green!

CHAPTER 7

A Better Arrangement

"Arranging a bowl of flowers in the morning can give a sense of quiet in a crowded day – like writing a poem or saying a prayer."
– Anne Morrow Lindbergh

Now that you've de-cluttered and gotten yourself in the "green groove," it's time to get down to the business of rearranging your home and creating the space of your dreams. In this chapter, I'll take you through some of the rooms and areas in your home and give you pointers on how to position furniture and other features to create a living space that enhances your life to the fullest. When assessing a room, think about the energy flow and how it feels when you enter. Are there areas where it is hard to walk because the furniture is crowded? If you have trouble walking past something, that's a clear sign that the energy flow isn't what it could be.

Let's begin...

Front Entrance

This is the first impression you get of your space every time you come home. It is also the first impression others have of your home, so it is especially important for it to feel inviting. Ensure that it is easy for anyone to walk up to your front door. Remove or prune back bushes, trees or plants that might be blocking your door area. Add a plant or two to the outside of your home, one on either side, if you want. Fake plants are okay if your climate won't support real plants during some seasons (just make sure you keep them looking clean and nice).

Make sure the door functions well (handle works, door opens and closes properly, doorbell works). Add a "welcome" sign or welcome mat. Incorporate the color red into your front entrance — you can paint the door red if you like, or just have some red in your welcome sign or mat. The color red helps to encourage the

Plants and flowers are an incredible way to say welcome, and they encourage an abundance of positive energy. Use a variety of evergreens and potted flowers depending on your climate so that you always have some form of life at your front door.

flow of wealth and prosperity energy into the home. Feel good about your entrance and others will feel good too when they enter your home.

Now walk in the door. Take a look around. Is it dark and gloomy, or fresh and bright? Is it hard to get in the door because there is stuff wedged in behind it? When you walk into your home, you should be greeted with a feeling of openness. This means a lack of clutter: shoes, jackets, hats and mitts should be stored away in closets with the doors closed, organized so they can be accessed easily. Make sure the foyer is clean, swept and organized. Hang pictures in the entrance area that make you feel peaceful when you come home and inspire you as you embark on every new adventure.

Avoid hanging mirrors directly across from the doorway, as this will reflect energy right back out the door. If your front entryway and your back entryway are directly in line with each other, the energy will come in one door and go straight out the other, which is not desirable, and is difficult to change. If this is the case, add some plants or hang a wind chime or crystal in between the two doors to slow down the flow of energy and keep it within your home. If you have a staircase that leads straight up or down from one of your outside entrances, hang a wind chime or crystal in between the stairs and the door. This will slow the energy that would normally rush up or down the stairs and out of the home.

Wealth Corner

If you have not yet done the Bagua grid home-mapping exercise from Chapter 3, stand at your front door looking into your home. Determine where the far left corner is and place three coins and something red in that area. Gold or silver coins will work. I recommend using three of the same coin but feel free to put whatever you like there. I have my coins on the windowsill, along with a small, pretty piece of red ribbon. It's important that no one moves these items, so you'll need to choose your spot wisely, especially if you have children or pets.

Notice in this picture the need to step a bit to the left to move easily into this entryway. The energy is slightly slowed, and it makes you feel just a bit awkward.

Notice how moving the bench creates an easier entry into this home. The addition of a rounded edge table helps encourage positive energy. A plant and a pair of Chinese Protector Lions (also called Foo/Fu Dogs) ensure that the energy coming into this home is only positive, welcoming, and loving.

Here is the main wealth corner in my home. I have a beautiful plant, a small red and gold Chinese envelope with money in it, a pretty blue ribbon, a small satchel of coins, and of course tomatoes! Tidy and out of the way just enough on the windowsill so that it will not to be questioned or touched. This corner of our home protects and grows our wealth every day.

Add a plant in a red pot and a water fountain if you have space for it. Water is an amazing way to increase positive energy. If you do not have a fountain, you can just use a dish with water in it. Just be sure to change the water frequently, as dirty, stagnant water can have the opposite effect of what you are intending to achieve. Pay attention to what happens to your wealth and prosperity once you have taken these steps.

I also like to "pump up" the wealth corner on my desk (far left corner from the front of the desk) with the same items, as my desk is a reflection of my career. Add things like a picture of your company logo if you want to increase your business wealth, or a piece of paper describing your financial goals inside a red envelope. Doing these things lets the Universe know what you want.

Living Room

Organize furniture in your living room so that it is conducive to good conversation. Placing your sofa and chairs across from each other, or in a round-ish pattern, allows those seated on them to see each other's faces. Make sure it is easy to walk around the whole living room without banging your knees on tables or chairs. Put plants in the corners and, of course, remove any clutter!

Dining Room

Make your dining room a place where your family and friends will want to sit, relax and enjoy a delicious meal together. Show the importance of dining together by setting the table attractively for meals and using your good plates and china on a regular basis. Use flowers and candles for centerpieces to encourage family and guests to linger at the table beyond the actual meal.

When the food is finished, clear the dirty dishes to the kitchen as quickly as possible and then return to the table to keep guests socializing. Serve tea or coffee after dinner, let the kids run and play and enjoy the time with your guests, or your loved ones. All too often, meals are seen as something to be rushed through so we can pack more activity into our busy lifestyles. Take the time to enjoy your meal and consider it an opportunity to catch up with your kids, husband, friends and family.

Bedrooms

Your bedroom should be a space where you can go and feel all the troubles of the day melt away. It should be an area in your home where there is not a lot of external stimulation to take your mind away from feeling relaxed. This will help you to stimulate other areas in your life that you should be focused on in the bedroom… like sleeping!

The placement of your bed is the key to a peaceful, restful and healthy sleep. When you are lying in your bed, you should be able to see the door of the room just by lifting up your head. The reasoning behind this is that by allowing an easy view of the door, no one can sneak up on you. Your feet should not be pointing directly at the door and the door should not be pointing directly at your head.

If you are standing at the door of your room, the best placement of your bed is with the headboard on the opposite wall, offset to one side of the door. Your headboard should be up against a firm wall and there should be ample space to walk around either side of the bed. There should be nothing underneath your bed at all. Clutter under the bed is thought to be detrimental to your health and your finances, so move anything that is under there out immediately!

If you have a bed with storage drawers underneath, it is imperative that you keep everything in there neatly folded and tidy.

To promote relaxation in the bedroom, get rid of any and all electronics. Having a TV in the bedroom is very bad Feng Shui for several reasons. First of all the energy given off by electronics is negative in nature and harmful to your physical health. Secondly, TV is very stimulating to the mind and watching TV right before bed can cause insomnia, bad dreams, worry, anxiety and general restlessness. In our bedrooms we want to let go of the day and allow the subconscious to work on our future dreams and goals while we are sleeping. This can only happen when we feel truly relaxed and peaceful.

If you insist on watching TV before bed, make sure to stop watching at least a half hour before you go to sleep. I would recommend watching your show, then brushing your teeth, washing your face and hopping into bed with a good book. Try to read for a minimum of 15 minutes before sleeping. This will distract your mind from the stimulation of the TV and it will also distract your thoughts from the events of the day. If you absolutely must have a TV in your room, enclose it in a cupboard with doors so that the harmful rays are not shooting out at you through the night, or cover it with fabric before you go to sleep.

Enjoying the relaxing effects of your bedroom before you fall asleep can also help to stimulate your life between the sheets. Ladies, we all know that we have to be in the right frame of mind to "get in the mood." If we are stressed out, anxious or worried about things that happened during the day, there is usually no way that we're going to be up for any other bed-based activities, no matter what kind of tricks our men have up their sleeves. Men, on the other hand, do not appear to struggle with this quite as much.

If you give yourself 15 minutes of relaxing reading in bed (without falling asleep with your book on your chest) you may be surprised at the improvement in your mood, and your man will likely start coming to bed to "relax" along with you.

As the bedroom is the place for nurturing your love relationship, there are a few simple ways that you can use Feng Shui to stimulate this area of your life. Have pairs of things in your bedroom instead of single things. For example, place matching side tables with matching lamps on them on either side of your bed. Hang art that displays pairs of things. Have a pair of candles or a pair of chairs. Remove all clutter from your bedroom. Keep just one or two books in your room — one that you are currently reading and maybe the next one that you want to read. Your side tables should otherwise be clear of other items and your dresser tops and tabletops should be as clear and neat as possible.

Do not bring work into the bedroom! You spend enough time thinking about work during the day, so make this room a refuge and an escape. Put away as much as you can into cupboards, closets and drawers and allow yourself to enjoy the relaxing effects that a clear space can give. Make your bed and open up the curtains every morning. I am not trying to nag at you, but just doing this small task has a huge effect on your daily mindset. You are subconsciously saying that you like yourself by providing a clean, neat, relaxing space. When you come home at night, that space will be lovingly waiting for you.

In this room, the bed is messy, the stickers are cluttering the walls, there is laundry on the floor, and too many things on the nightstands. Leaving your room in this state can give you anxious feelings all through the day!

Small things can make huge differences. Notice in this picture that the bed is neatly made, side tables are tidy, and 2 plants have been added on either side. The plants cover up the unsightly electrical sockets and cords, and lessen the negative effect of electrical energy. Notice the duplicity in this bedroom...2 side tables, 2 plants, 2 lamps. This is the kind of bedroom that welcomes you home and allows you to relax, refresh, unwind, and have fun!

Do not leave dirty laundry lying on the floor. In fact, do not leave anything lying on the floor! Laundry should be kept in a basket or hamper in your closet or laundry room until you get around to doing it. I've said it before and I'll say it again: Living in a home that is neat and organized will make you feel amazing!

Allow new love to enter into your life by getting rid of items that remind you of past romantic relationships. If you have pictures of old lovers around, or mementos that remind you of that relationship, get rid of them. Your mind will see these items and mentally keep you in the past. Once you have gotten rid of these items, your mind will instantly allow for exciting new loves. Let go of the past, and get excited about the future.

Kids Bedrooms

As with any bedroom, this room should be a sanctuary for restful sleep. Toys should not be kept in the bedroom, unless they are contained in a closet or toy chest. Having toys in the room is stimulating to children, making it harder for them to settle down at night, and making their sleep less restful. Teach your children the value of having an organized, clean bedroom. Books are also stimulating, so try to keep them in the closet or nicely organized on a bookshelf. Get your kids their own laundry basket and keep that in the closet as well, encouraging them to put their dirty clothing in themselves. By teaching kids the value of keeping things neat and tidy in their own space, you are helping to generate positive energy in their lives now and in the future.

Bathrooms

Wealth energy is sucked down the drains of toilets, showers and sinks. If you want to improve your financial situation it is very important to keep the toilet lid down. This may be a hard one for the guys in your life, but once you convince them that their money will go down the toilet if they don't comply, you're guaranteed to see an immediate improvement.

Your children will benefit from having a tidy, peaceful sleeping area where stimulation is kept to a minimum. Here, a plant has been added to the wealth corner, and something red has been hung from the ceiling in that corner. The child's piggy bank is also placed in this location and will ensure prosperity. Teach your children the value of organization, efficiency and energy flow. These are valuable life skills.

You can go so far as to block your shower drains with a plastic cover, or, at the very least make sure that the shower door or curtain is kept closed at all times. Bathroom doors should always be kept closed as well. At the start, you may find yourself making these adjustments for others and constantly having to remind them to follow suit. Instead of being upset about it, try to think about all the wealth that you are protecting!

Keep bathroom countertops as clear as possible. Put everything you can away in cupboards or drawers. It sounds a little daunting, but again, if everything has a place, keeping it off the counter will be easy and will make you feel good. Add a plant or two to the bathroom, preferably close to the toilet. Plants help to absorb the negative energy that is generated in bathrooms.

Clean the hair out of your brush every time you use it. This only takes a second and makes such a difference in how you feel when you use your brush again. For a long time, I did not do this and ended up throwing out a lot of brushes. By cleaning it regularly, I've found it really easy to keep a brush clean, even with three daughters who all have long hair. It just goes to show that if you take time to do little things consistently, you'll reap rewards in the long run.

Adding a plant to your bathroom can really help reduce the negative energy that emanates from these areas.

Furniture

When it comes to selecting furniture, rounded edges are always better than pointy, sharp edges. Always choose round or oval tables over rectangular/square tables. Round tables are much better when it comes to stimulating conversation, particularly with a big group. You will also have fewer injuries from people inevitably bumping themselves against the tables (kids are especially bad for this, but adults also ram their shins or bump their hips from time to time).

If the furniture you currently own is not rounded, don't think that you have to go out and buy all new items, just consider this for future purchases. There are things you can do to work with what you've got. For example: pointy hard edges can be tamed by adding a tablecloth, which improves the energy from the corners immensely. There really is a cure for everything and spending a ton of money is not the goal!

Plants

Plants are an amazing and easy way to add life, energy, balance and health to your home, and they look fantastic in every room, as well as outside and inside the entryway. Corners give off negative energy (in Feng Shui, this is referred to as "poisoned arrows"), so placing plants in the corners of your home can significantly improve the energy in those rooms. If you are focused on improving your financial situation, putting a plant in a red pot in your wealth corner can significantly affect that area of your life. If you want to stimulate your love life, put a plant with pink flowers in your love/marriage corner. To improve your job prospects place a plant in a black pot somewhere in your career center. Ribbons are a fast and easy way to add color. Tying a ribbon around a plant pot looks cute and fun.

Principles of Feng Shui say to avoid having prickly cactus plants in the home, as they are sharp, dangerous and do not promote good energy. Instead, choose plants with smooth, round leaves. The jade plant is known as the "Chinese Money" plant, making it great choice for the wealth corner of your home. Bamboo, schefelera, dieffenbachia and ficus are also believed to be good plants to have in your home. Recently, I learned that the Peace Lily (spathiphyllum) is a plant that is superb at cleaning the air of pollutants. It has nice leaves and grows beautiful white flowers. It is also not a finicky plant, so even those without green thumbs should be able to care for these little guys.

Really, if you ask me, I'd say any plant is a good plant and the more the better (except if they start to look cluttered, of course!)

Adding a plant to this corner of the room softens the negative energy given off by the corner while also providing stability to the chair. Furniture that cannot be directly up against the firmness of a wall should be grounded with a plant behind it.

Lighting

Lighting is extremely important. The levels of lighting in each room in your home can have a dramatic effect on your mood. When lighting is soft and dim, it will make you feel calm. Candlelight can make you feel sensuous and romantic. Candles can also make an ordinary dinner elegant and special. When every bright light in your house is on, it can make you feel over-stimulated, intense, and anxious. Be conscious of the lighting in your home. When you are ready to relax at the end of the day, turn the lights down in order to prepare your mind. If you want to increase the likelihood of some romance in your life, use candles. Use lighting to set a dinner party mood. Use a disco ball and some low-level lamps when you are having a rockin' party for a fun, nightclub vibe. Recognize how lighting makes you feel and use it to your advantage.

Artwork and Accessories

Art and other decorative things in the home should inspire you and make you feel calm and happy. If you do not like something about a particular picture or piece, get rid of it. Train yourself to feel the energy that objects give off. Only keep, or buy, things that give you a truly positive feeling. If you have artworks in your home that have been given to you by others and you do not like them, you need to get rid of them. It's not personal. By getting rid of the item, you are not saying: "I don't like you." Rather, you are simply being assertive about what you like, and since you did not choose it for yourself, you can feel free to have your own opinion. Remember, you are the one living in your home. Take control, be strong and don't be swayed by feelings of obligation. Inspire yourself everyday with your surroundings.

"The book is now a part of my life. It has fueled my obsession with keeping things tidy. I need the book in all parts of my life and I want more! I even found myself organizing the moving boxes in the basement! It's like I can hear her in my head. After the Go Green chapter I put a ziplock bag in the garbage and immediately it was like she was holding my hand and forcing me to pick it back out. Thanks from a true fan."

CHAPTER 8

Do It, Do It, Do It!

"You can't stay in your corner of the forest waiting for others to come to you. You have to go to them sometimes."
– A.A. Milne

Getting your entire house uncluttered, organized and arranged in accordance with the life-enhancing philosophies of Feng Shui takes time. Once you've achieved this, unless you consciously maintain it, you'll be right back where you started. It's time to talk about: "cleaning as you go" and "doing it now."

"Clean as you go" was the motto on the wall of the Dairy Queen that I worked at for my first job, and I still use this today. When you are cooking, put things away as you are done with them, don't wait until you are done cooking or your kitchen will become cluttered and inefficient. Maintain your uncluttered space on an ongoing basis, and it will never take very long to get it right back the way it should be, which brings me to my next success law: Do it NOW!

I will admit that I take the concept of "Do it now" to a whole new level. I am passionate about organizing to the point of being slightly obsessive-compulsive, annoying and, yes, a bit "pushy" too. If something is bugging me, I will be overcome by a crazy urge to change it, as my cousin Julie in Ontario can attest. On one of my visits, she and I were sitting together at the kitchen table, having a very emotional conversation. From where I was sitting, I could see that the living-room layout was just not right. I abruptly got up from the table, telling her: "You have got to change that! The energy is just not flowing well in there!"

I then proceeded to start moving things around. Good thing my cousin was so willing to let me do my thing because when I feel this kind of urge, I get truly excited and can't put things off. I have to start "doing it now" because I know with all my heart that the changes I am making are going to make a big difference.

This sort of thing is also known to happen during the weekly Wednesday lunches at my sister Brenda's house. If Brenda says something like: "I've been thinking about changing the living room around..." I'm in there like a dirty shirt. I just love to see results. It got to the point that Brenda was planning out reorganization projects she wanted us do every Wednesday. The good thing is that these days, I can relax for the most part because we have done almost every room in the house. We are an amazing team!

Just recently, I convinced my own business coach to move 75 file boxes out of his office. These boxes were cluttering the space, affecting his business — and mine — in a negative way (as far as energy goes, anyways). It took me a few weeks to win him over, but I stood firm. I pitched in myself and even brought in my own management team to help him move the boxes. I have also been guilty of spontaneously cleaning someone else's kitchen while I am at their house. Is That Girl obsessive-compulsive? Only if it negatively affects her life, which, in my case, I can assure you it doesn't!

But let's talk about your home now, and let's start with the kitchen. When you come home from work at night, you should be coming home to a clean kitchen that is ready for you to cook dinner. In order to have that, you have to plan to leave your kitchen neat before you leave for work in the morning. So much to do, so little time? Not so! Let me help you with this simple plan:

Every night before you allow yourself to go and relax in front of the TV or read your book, take a walk around your house. Make sure all the dishes are done in the kitchen, and if you let them air dry, take a minute to put them away just before you go to bed or dry them and put them away immediately. Pack tomorrow's lunches and put them in the fridge. Ensure all the countertops in the kitchen are free of clutter and are clean. Put everything away that you can. Run the dishwasher if it's full, so that it will be done by the time your show is over and you can unload it that evening. Get out coffee (or tea) mugs for the morning, prepare the coffee so you can just push the "on" button (or get a tea bag and kettle ready), take bread out of the freezer for toast and take the butter out of the fridge so it will be easy to spread (or, if your family eats something else for breakfast, do what you can to make it similarly accessible and easy to prepare).

If you are low on any groceries like milk or bread or fruit, write it down on a piece of paper and keep that by your purse so you can remember it for the next day. Decide what you would like to prepare for dinner the following day and get out your cookbook (if you need one). If your meal requires meat, take it out of the freezer and put it in the fridge to thaw. Check the recipe and make sure you have all of the ingredients, if not, add whatever's missing to the grocery list so you can pick it up on your way home from work the next day. Meal planning can seem like an overwhelming task. Luckily, there are tools out there to help make it easier. Check out any of Sandi Richard's amazing *Cooking for the Rushed* cookbooks, which bring together recipes, meal planning and grocery list making in one great book. My hairdresser introduced me to these books back when they were first released and I've been using them ever since. Seriously, Sandi can make anyone look like a pro!

Before you walk away from the kitchen in the evening, take a look at the breakfast table and make sure it is clean and neat. Then do a quick walk around the house and pick up anything on the floor that can be put away. Make sure all the kids' toys are put away and the mail is in its rightful spot so you can deal with it at an appropriate time. Hang up any jackets tossed over the railing by the front door and put away any shoes left out by the entrance.

You must train yourself to be a stickler about putting things away, keeping cupboard doors closed and keeping your living space in "show-home ready" condition at all times. Understandably, there will be times when you will be too busy at night to get all of this done. If that's the case, plan to be up early and take care of things in the morning. If you know you have a busy night ahead of you, plan to get done as much as you can that morning, or even the night before.

Yes, this all requires some advance planning, but in the end, it only takes an hour or so of your time each day. This hour, which most people spend watching TV, can give you the jumpstart you need to feel prepared, be on time, and better enjoy your entire day — especially knowing that dinner is covered.

In the mornings, make your bed and your children's beds. Open up all the blinds and let the sunshine in. Leave your home in a peaceful state and you will be subconsciously peaceful through the day.

Clean as you go and do it now! It works, guaranteed.

CHAPTER 9

Time Is on Your Side (Yes It Is!)

"When it is obvious that the goals cannot be reached, don't adjust the goals, adjust the action steps."
— Confucius

All good things come in time. Efficiency is the ability to get the maximum done in the least amount of time. One of the key elements of efficiency is learning how to schedule the events in your life. It's important to keep a notebook or journal on you so that as soon as you think about something you can write it down, plan it and book it. To give you an example: I have our annual themed Halloween party planned and booked one year in advance. It's never too early!

A notebook is also important to keep track of your thoughts — you never know when inspiration might strike. When your brain starts running with your next great idea or action plan, take a second to jot things down. Your ideas are amazing, but you may be in the middle of something else and you can't do everything all at once. Writing things down as they come to mind relieves the anxiety you may have about forgetting those important thoughts! As more time becomes available, you can go back and review your notebook and decide what your next priority should be.

Here are some tried-and-true time-management tips that I use everyday:

- Create a daily schedule for yourself that is broken down into half-hour increments. You can buy an agenda that is laid out this way, or if you are impatient like me and want to "do it now," print out a daily calendar from Outlook or another computer program and keep your day sheets in a three-ring binder. This system will allow you to keep track of pretty much everything you do over the course of the day.
- Keep your schedule binder with you at all times. You can make "to-do" lists and notes right there on each day's page. This allows you to see exactly what kind of time you have in a day to schedule the appointments, events and activities that need to get done.
- In order to feel prepared and on-track, schedule even simple household chores and other everyday activities. Things like laundry, making lunches and dinners and getting groceries should all be in the schedule. Include driving time and try to be realistic about what you can actually get done in a day. Hair appointments, work hours, workouts, play dates, lunches, vacations, volunteer days and deadlines should all be in there. *Everything* you do in a day should be on your list. This includes work, family and personal time.
- Do not use two different calendars. It is way too hard to keep track of both!
- Set your mind at ease by reviewing the next day before you go to bed at night. Perhaps at this point you'll notice an extra hour somewhere. What are you going to do with that hour? Is it enough time to squeeze in a trip to the grocery store? Would

you rather get a quick pedicure, or just relax and read a book? Perhaps it would be a good time to take care of something with an upcoming deadline like renewing your driver's license.

You *will* have the time to do everything you want if you learn to schedule your time. If you find that you are just simply not able to complete certain tasks, or it seems you never have enough time, then it's possible you do not want the result of that task bad enough. Results come through actions, and sometimes we have to do things that we do not like in order to get the desired results. Prioritize your tasks according to how quickly you want to see results. Write down what you need to do and then do it now! Be accountable to yourself and do not let yourself down. Of course, this means you will have to be reasonable about how much you can get done in a day. There is only so much time. If you are being realistic, however, you should be able to fit in whatever you need to do as long as you do not waste your time.

Any binder can work as your agenda.

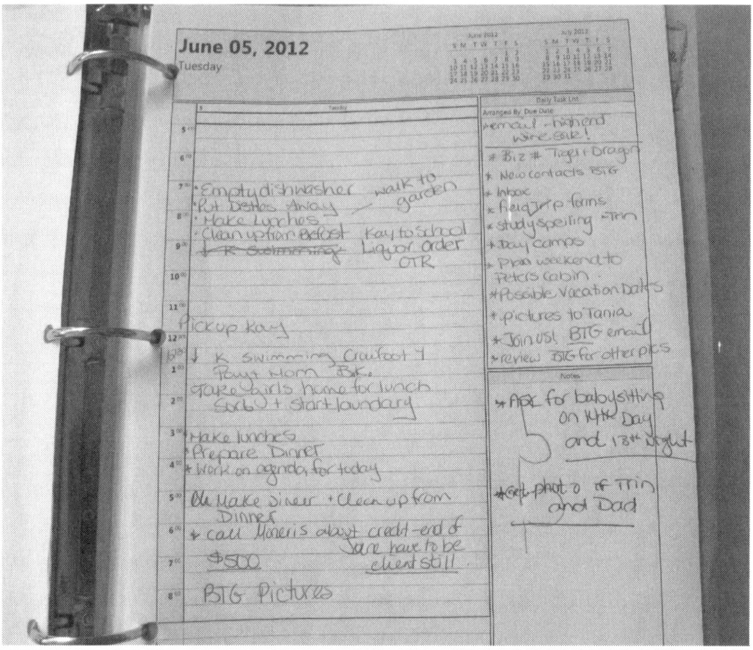

This is an actual page from my own agenda. I have everything written down including doing laundry, meal preparation, work stuff, and to-do items. Seeing your day written like this before the actual day happens can really make you feel prepared, and will help you see where you can squeeze in other chores. Reviewing your week after it has happened (as long as you have written everything down) can be an effective way to assess your own performance and time going forward.

It's also important to schedule in your own personal time. Do not wait until everything else is scheduled to put yourself on the calendar or you will find that you never have time for yourself. You do need to be selfish sometimes and take care of you. Being That Girl requires some effort, so you need to ensure that you are taking care of yourself and keeping yourself energetic. Make yourself important and give yourself time on the calendar. And do not feel guilty about this! You are the only one that can make you feel guilty about taking time for yourself, so let go of that feeling. It does not matter what others think of you. Life is not a popularity contest, but a happiness contest. It's great to always be thinking of others, but we need to enter ourselves into the happiness contest too.

Change is inevitable, and life is often unpredictable, but on the whole, humans do best when life has some structure to it. Humans like having things scheduled. As soon as you think: "Oh, I should really do that," (like "I should plan that birthday party," or "I should really call someone about that," or "I should clean out my fridge") write this intention down in your agenda or notebook. This will take it out of your head and get you working on it right away. I feel like I can't emphasize this enough!

Set deadlines for yourself, otherwise you'll never have a reason to get things done because, really, most of what we do can always be done later. If you set a date for when you want something completed, you will know how much time you have to complete it and you can start breaking that project down in terms of how much you have to get done every day, every week and every month to reach your goal. If you set a date, do everything in your power to stick to it. You need to be accountable to your goals.

Financial management is also important when it comes to being efficient. Learn how to set a budget. To do this, all you need to know is how much you make or bring in every month and how much your set expenses are, and then how much your variable expenses are. You do not need a fancy Excel spreadsheet to create a budget. Just a simple ledger book or worksheet works just as well. The goal is to have your monthly income exceed (be more than) the monthly expenses. Any excess money that you have should go into savings. If your expenses are more than your monthly income, then you are going into debt and you will need to change something — you'll either have to increase your income, decrease your expenses, or do both in order to come out ahead. Decide what is really important to you and figure out a way to have what you want. If you need to pay down debt, you are going to need extra income each month to do that. Make it happen. It is all within your control.

Utilizing a budget worksheet is the key to knowing where you are financially today. It can also help you plan for the future. On the following page, you will see a worksheet that is easily laid out and

Be That Girl Budget Worksheet

MONTHY HOUSEHOLD INCOME			
	Expected	Actual	Difference
Your Wage			
Partners Wage			
Misc. Income			
TOTAL INCOME			

MONTHY HOUSEHOLD EXPENSES			
	Expected	Actual	Difference
SAVINGS:			
Personal Savings			
RESP/RRSP Contributions			
HOME:			
Mortgage/Rent			
Property Tax			
Insurance			
Maintenance			
Electricity			
Water			
Heat			
Phone			
TRANSPORTATION:			
Car Payment			
Insurance			
Fuel			
Maintenance			
Transit Pass			
CHILD CARE:			
School Fees			
Babysitter			
Activities			
Food:			
Groceries			
Restaurants			
PERSONAL:			
Clothing			
Shoes			
Accessories			
HEALTH CARE:			
Premium			
Hair & Nail Care			
Make-Up			
Gym Membership			
ENTERTAINMENT:			
Alcohol			
Movies			
MISC. EXPENSES:			
TOTAL EXPENSES			

Total Income – Total Expenses	
Total Actual Income	
Total Actual Expenses	
TOTAL:	

*Any positive amount in your total is the amount of extra cashflow you will have every month. Decide where you will put it.

*If the amount in your total is zero, you are running on a balanced budget. No extras on top of your budget allowed.

*Any negative amount in your total is the amount you are going into debt every month. Time to assess your expenses ready for you to use. You will also find a downloadable Personal Budget Worksheet on my website at **www.bethatgirlnow.com**.

It is crucial that you pay all your bills on time. If you are not set up for Internet banking, now is the time to do that. It is a real timesaver when it comes to paying bills. Setting up preauthorized payments for your monthly bills is another way to save time and ensure that payments happen on time. If you have budgeted properly for your expenses, there will always be funds available to pay your bills.

It is also important to get in the habit of rewarding yourself when you make a positive change in your life that ends up saving you money: quitting smoking, for example. My husband and I had both started smoking in our teens, and we made the decision to quit together. When we quit, a pack of cigarettes cost $6-$7. That, to us, was a lot of money (since then, these little cancer sticks have increased to more than $10 per pack). With the money we saved from kicking that bad habit to the curb, we decided to reward ourselves by hiring a housecleaner to come every two weeks. We figured we could handle the everyday tidying and organizing and then have someone else handle the nitty-gritty. We have had someone cleaning for us ever since. When we were smoking, we always found money for cigarettes. Now we always find money to have someone help us keep our house clean. This is a major reward for us, and a much healthier way to spend that money! If you're a smoker, when you quit (and you will) make sure you do something special with your cigarette money too.

My husband and I also believe that having someone clean for us is a way of placing a value on our time. We could be spending a whole day every two weeks cleaning our home, or we could be out having fun as a family. To us, a day together is worth much more than what we pay someone to do the cleaning. Think about how much you value your own time and then make smart decisions about how to spend your time based on that valuation. We all work hard; increase your happiness by playing hard too. Remember, money should not be the only thing that counts.

If you have more free time for yourself and more time to help others you won't necessarily see an increase in your bank balance, but certainly these things are their own rewards.

Every activity that you have completed in this book so far (Five Year Plan-making, organizing your home, cleaning as you go, and doing it now) has been designed to help you prioritize your time and have you managing your time more efficiently. When you are organized, calm and efficient, you will find more time and energy to focus you on chasing your passions.

Let's keep it rolling!

CHAPTER 10

The Infinite Universe

"Faith is a passionate intuition."
– William Wordsworth

I must start off this chapter by saying that I was not raised in a family that practiced any organized religion, nor was my family very spiritual in any sense of the word. I did not attend church or go to a school that focused on any particular religion. Even so, I felt independently inclined toward spirituality at a young age. I attended Sunday school with my friends and came away thinking it was the best thing ever. All the people there had something in common, a shared belief in something amazing. This idea was very attractive to me. I began to explore my spirituality on my own and was always on the lookout for "signs." I always felt that there was something much greater than us "out there," guiding us in a certain direction, pushing us here, holding us back there, and providing us with the information we need to succeed if we could figure out how to listen.

Today, I refer to this force simply as "the Universe" and I believe we have the power to tap into it for guidance. When we recognize this, we can make incredible things happen for our families and ourselves. This is a very powerful idea, and I understand that it might sound a bit far out, but have faith and keep reading, and soon you will be using the power of the Universe to achieve whatever you want too.

When I was a teenager, a friend introduced me to a book called *The Celestine Prophecy* by author James Redfield. This book was one of my first introductions to how the strange little coincidences in life can be explained. I have not read the book again since then, yet it continues to have a powerful influence in shaping my perceptions.

This book truly opened up my mind to a whole new Universe, one that I had some control over. The most important thing that I took from it, the thing that has stuck with me up until now and

You never know when you will be inspired! While cleaning up during a kindergarten volunteer day, I noticed this magnet randomly placed on a paper towel roll. The Universe will give you signs if you are watching carefully!

will stick with me over the course of my lifetime, is that *there are no coincidences*. Everything in life happens for a reason, and if you are open and ready you will always be given what you need.

We have all experienced what we would call "coincidences." Have you ever found yourself thinking about someone you haven't seen in years and then suddenly within the next week you see him or her again? Have you ever thought about something specific, for example: "I wish I knew where to find someone good to teach violin to my daughter..." You ponder this in your mind. Technically, you are looking for a concrete answer and you know you could just go on the Internet to find this information, but maybe you just haven't had the time to do that, and even if you do have time, you don't know if the person you find will be good.

The next day at school maybe you are talking to one of the other moms and she happens to mention that her own daughter had violin lessons the previous night. Of course, you immediately ask where she takes her daughter and if she is happy with the quality of instruction... Suddenly, you have the information you need. Coincidence? Not exactly. It's just the Universe providing for you. The key is being willing and able to listen while having conversations with people and actively providing them with information about what you need.

The truth is that you have already been given, and you will continue to be given, everything you need to succeed, but you have to be open, ready, and willing to receive what you need, or you will miss it. Always be looking for an opportunity to help others while also helping yourself. If you are focused on this, you will become a much better listener and also a much more engaging conversationalist.

Listen intently for selfish reasons and provide information for altruistic reasons. Look people in the eye when you are listening to them and try to assess their body language. Doing this will help you listen better and you will also be able to "hear" the unspoken things that people are communicating. You will be amazed at the information that you receive and others will be amazed by you in return!

I actively ask the Universe for things and am not shy to say these requests out loud. My regional manager at On the Rocks can confirm the following story (as well as many other accounts of what she at first considered pretty weird behavior). I was actively pursuing a location for a new store and was getting frustrated at what appeared to be a lack of progress. In front of my regional manager, I looked up and said out loud: "I really need something to happen with this new store today. I just really need someone to call me back, please!" No joke, my cell phone started ringing within 10 minutes. I was overjoyed!

Now, it does not always happen that quickly, but it *will* happen if you really put your mind to it. One important thing to understand is that if you want something to happen, or you want to achieve a goal, you cannot just ask the Universe to provide for you and then sit back and do nothing. You must actively pursue the goal and put the necessary effort in. Along the way, ask the Universe to help guide you, to help make things happen quicker and easier. This is not "magic." It is simply believing in yourself and believing that you have the power to make anything happen (with the help of the Universe, of course). The true power is within you. The true power is you!

When you are focused on a goal, you may find yourself getting caught up in the day-to-day processes required to achieve that goal. In your mind, you might have a definite idea of how things are supposed to happen in order to get to your desired goal. The fact is, things do not always happen the way we think they will.

Throughout your life, you are going to run into roadblocks. You will be humming along, taking action and getting results, when, all of a sudden, there will be a stopper thrown at you. Something will not go your way and it is going to frustrate you.

I want to encourage you to "go with the flow" a little when it comes to your goals. Stay focused on the prize and never stop taking action. If you are trying everything in your power and you keep running into roadblocks, perhaps it is time to move on to something else or try something different. Do not just keep doing the same things if they are not working.

The Universe works in mysterious ways, and at times it will be telling you NOT to proceed with your current plan. If you are pursuing a path and nothing is working, don't be upset. There is a reason that it is not supposed to go that way and you need to embrace that and move on to something else.

When I am pursuing something, if it is fairly easy and things just seem to fall into place (not by magic but because of the effort I am putting in) I take this as a sign that I am on the right path. When things consistently do not go the way I have planned, I still get very upset. I like it when things go my way, but eventually I embrace the idea that this time, it was not supposed to work out for a reason.

When Ryan and I were attempting to purchase our second liquor store, we found what we believed was a great location in a good neighborhood. We came to an agreement with the owners and started looking into financing. No matter what we did, we just were not able to finance the deal. We later found out that the owners had not been providing us with accurate financial information.

After that deal fell through, I kept looking for a second store. I picked up the phone and called all of the existing stores that I considered to be in good locations and asked if they wanted to sell (do not be afraid to make "cold calls" or ask questions of people you do not know. Be confident enough not to take rejection personally and you will reap the rewards from this technique). As it turned out, another store in the same neighborhood as our first store was interested in selling, so we were able to add that store to the On the Rocks group. This store was a much better location — essentially, we ended up buying our competition! We would have missed this excellent opportunity if the previous deal had been a go. The Universe was looking out for us the whole time.

What I'm trying to say here is that sometimes it's best to step back a bit and have faith if things don't seem to be progressing the way you expect. You will be given what you need when you need it, and you will be steered in another direction when it is required. Don't fight too hard; instead, try to go with the flow. Embrace the good and the bad and stay focused on your goal. You will get there, even if it doesn't happen the way you envisioned. Enjoy the journey: the ups, downs and turnarounds. You'll get there with the help of the Universe, no matter what path you end up taking.

Recognize that the Universe provides and convince yourself of this by watching for those "coincidences." Every time you experience one of these so-called coincidences, your faith will grow. Once you are truly convinced (which means you have faith) you will be able to tap into the infinite power of the Universe. As I mentioned before, I frequently "look up" and ask for guidance and help from the Universe, and because I have faith, the Universe provides exactly what I am looking for. Soon, you will be able to manifest everything and anything you want.

Be thankful to the Universe when things do go as planned. Look up and express your gratitude. Being appreciative of what you have will ensure that more of that goodness is sent your way. When opportunities are presented to you that live up to all of your standards and expectations, give yourself a pat on the back, because *you* created that.

Let me give you an example from my own life. About three years ago, I had a dream about a big, white house. Six months after that dream, Ryan and I sat down to write our revised Five Year Plan. That plan included: "move to a private, treed acreage with lots of space."

Shortly afterwards, we made an appointment with our banker and found out what we could afford if we were to pursue purchasing another home.

We started causally looking at real estate in our price range. Our realtor sent us a bunch of listings in an area that appealed to us. I looked through them first, and then Ryan looked through them on his own. There was one listing that both of us agreed we just had to go and see — a big, white house that had everything we were looking for.

BE THAT GIRL

Opportunities will come to you if you are asking for things and if you are observant enough to recognize opportunity. It is what you choose to do with opportunity that can really set you apart from others.

Of course, we chose to look at other homes too, but we were most excited about the white house. We actually looked at that house last, and it truly was perfect. Absolutely, divinely perfect.

We bought it and have been living there ever since. Even the numeric address of this house was almost an exact match to the home phone number that we have had for almost 15 years. Coincidence? There are no coincidences.

I want you to take one of the goals from the Five Year Plan you created as part of the "Planet Do It" chapter and break it down into small steps, or smaller goals. If you want to take a trip to Italy, for example, there are several things you are going to need to do to get there:

Figure Out The Budget For The Trip

- Check into flights using an online flight-booking system to gauge what it is going to cost.
- Look into accommodations and decide what your budget is for hotels or other types of lodging.
- Figure out a reasonable daily budget for food. This budget will be different for everyone. Base it on what you would like to be doing/eating while you are there.

Start Planning An Itinerary

- Internet chat boards and other sites that allow comments from fellow travelers are a great resource to help you decide on places to stay (and to avoid), what to do and other cool tips and tricks. Find someone who has similar interests based on what they recommend and then follow their lead. Ryan and I did this for our own trip to Italy and it worked like a charm. I am not one to spend hours doing research and making my own itineraries – I prefer to "poach and merge" whenever possible! We ended up on a great excursion to a small village where we ate lunch at a charming cantina, something we never would have even heard about if it weren't for that online recommendation. The instructions for the day trip were incredibly detailed, with train times, what to ask for at the cantina (in Italian), and then where to go to get affordable, good-quality (and yummy) wine to go with the food we purchased. It was so much fun!
- Figure out the best time(s) of year to travel based on what you want to do. Look at your own calendar and then decide on a time that will work for you and coincide with what you want to do on the trip. If there is a festival that you're dying to attend in September, then that's a good place to start.
- Buy yourself a travel guide and learn a few key phrases ("Where is the bathroom?" "What is this I'm eating?") before you arrive.

Start Saving Money

- Now that you have figured out how much money you're going to need and when you will be going, you can start planning how much you need to save each month in order to make the trip a reality. Let's say you plan to leave in September and it is March, and you need $5,000 to take the trip. That means you have to save $835 per month. I like to use my savings account for stuff like this. You can transfer money there as soon as it comes in and watch the balance grow.

- Find the money for your flight right away and book it! (Remember... Do it Now!) Even if you need to use your credit card at this point, I say do it! This will commit you to the trip and motivate you to earn or find the money to make it happen.
- Save up your bottle-refund money and ask your extended family if you can have theirs as donations.
- Remember all that clutter you cleared out of your home? Selling off your unwanted items can be a source of cash flow. Decide what is really important to you; a trip to Italy or a closet full of clothes you don't wear... Italy, or the Playstation you never use anymore... Italy or that motorbike in the garage... You get the picture!
- Work overtime, or pick up a part-time job to get a little extra money coming in, just for the short term.
- Ask for a raise at work because you deserve it! Perhaps you need to turn in a superstar performance for a couple of weeks before you ask, but do ask and you shall receive. Put the extra money towards your trip. Always ask for more than you're expecting because most employers like to negotiate you down. There's also a chance you may get the full amount you ask for! Just make sure you ask for that raise BEFORE you ask for the time off for your vacation.
- Go out less each month. Figure out what you would have spent on going out and put the money directly toward your trip.
- Allocate some money for your trip from every paycheck and put it directly into your savings account. You may choose to have this money automatically transferred from one account into your savings account. This "pay yourself first" approach will ensure you reach your goal as long as you don't touch that money.

Get Feng Shui Working For You

- Add some Italy paraphernalia to the travel center of your home or room: a postcard or picture of Italy, some Italian currency, anything that reminds you of your trip.

- Pump up the travel section with plants and pictures of your destination. Add objects that are metal, and use more black, grey and white in the travel section. This will really get the travel energy flowing!
- Pump up the energy in your wealth corner with plants, red items and more coins.

Ask the Universe to help you with each of these little plans. You will find that knowing what you need to do to reach your goal makes that goal more attainable and real. Plan it, then Do it! Be That Girl all around the world!

Speaking of being That Girl around the world, I am currently writing to you from a beautiful resort in Roatan, Honduras. The sun is shining, the waves are rolling in, and I am wearing my bathing suit and sipping a nice cold Barena beer. My three daughters are at home with my wonderful husband (thank you Ryan!) so that I can be on this journey of self-discovery. Let me tell you, it is definitely weird to wake up and not have someone wanting breakfast cooked, or needing their diaper changed! I planned this trip a week ago, and now here I am (thanks Dad!) Incredible!

Today, I have done yoga, checked my e-mail, swam in the pool three times, and am now working on this book. Other than that, I have no plans to rush anywhere. I've asked myself more than once: "How can I be doing this?"

I have three children, two retail stores, and a house on an acreage. How on earth am I living this dream of getting away and spending time by myself? Believe me when I tell you that the guilt I felt before this trip about leaving my children and my husband at home was intense. I have travelled with my husband before and left my children at home and the guilt was significantly less in that case.

Does my need for alone time or my quest for greater self-knowledge make me a horrible parent and a terrible wife? I think not. Now that I am here, I am reveling in the fact that I have gotten to a place with my stores that allows me to travel anytime I want. I am my own boss. I make the rules.

I have great people in place to handle things for me while I am away. My children are well adjusted and can function when one or both of their parents are not around. We are raising them to be independent young people, and they have enough self-confidence, intelligence and trust to be away from their parents as long as they are in the care of other great people that we trust.

For some of us, Being That Girl means Being That Mom — something that requires a book all its own! In the meantime, you'll find me stretched out on a lounge chair for just a little bit longer…

*"I loved being guided
into a mental/spiritual space
where I could push away all
the barriers and be wide open to think
big and wide and dream again."*

CHAPTER 11

Accentuate the Positive

"Your mind can only hold one thought at a time.
Make it a positive and constructive one."
– H. Jackson Brown, Jr.

In order to be successful at anything and everything, you must first believe that you can do it. Never start anything without first thinking: "I can do this." The first step toward realizing your success is convincing yourself that you are capable. You have to absolutely *adore* yourself and know that you really can do anything. That's all there is to it.

It sounds so simple, but this can be harder than it first appears. However, if you can master this concept, you really will be able to do anything. Now all we have to do is convince you of that!

BE THAT GIRL

It's not about where you've been, it's where you're going that matters.

Do you feel amazing about yourself? Do you know that you are incredible? If you cannot immediately answer: "Yes" to these questions, you are normal. Most people love themselves, but they have been trained not to like themselves. No matter who we are or what we have done in our lives, we all have a crazy, little negative voice in our heads. This voice constantly reminds us of all the bad, wrong, or silly things we have done. This is the voice that says things like:

"Stop thinking about all those crazy dreams!"

"You know you can't do that!"

"But..."

"How could I have been so stupid!?"

"I am such a bad person."

"Oh, it is so like me to do something like that!"

"Why does this always happen to me?"

"They don't like me. Look at them staring at me."

"They are all talking about me."

This negative voice has been with you for so long that it has become very sneaky. This voice can be screaming loudly at you and you still may not even realize it, since you have gotten so used to hearing it. This voice has an incredible power over you. Now is the time to stop this negative voice permanently and replace it with a much better voice.

Just as you have trained yourself to listen to this negative voice, you are now going to retrain your brain to focus on a new voice. Truthfully, it is not really a "new" voice at all. It's more like a voice that has always been there, but one that got ignored more and more over time. That positive voice says things to you like:

"Congratulations! I knew you could do it!"

"Of course you can do that! You can do anything!"

"You are amazing!"

"You go, Girl!"

"Wow! You sure turned that situation around!"

"What a great learning opportunity!"

"It's not personal."

"Just take care of you!"

"Stop worrying! You've got it all covered."

"I love you, and I like you."

Here is where the hard work begins. You are going to start changing which voice you listen to and, eventually, you will totally eliminate the negative voice. It will not be easy because the negative voice does not want to go away. It has been there with you for so long. How is it possible to just start ignoring it, you might be wondering? Here's how:

The following techniques can be used together or on their own. Pick and choose whichever you believe will work best. You may try something for a while and have great success and then suffer a setback. If you do suffer a setback, do not be hard on yourself! You are only human and it just means that you are having a positive effect on a negative behavior and that negative behavior is fighting back!

That said, I would recommend trying one thing and sticking with it wholeheartedly. As soon as that technique starts to lose its effectiveness, move on to the next one. You really can change the way your brain thinks and, if you can eliminate the negative voice, you will be able to tap into the infinite power of yourself and the Universe. This is going to be life-changing… I guarantee it!

1. Wear a thick elastic band on your left wrist. I prefer a beige-colored one as it draws less attention, but any color will do. Ultimately, I will wear whatever color I have on hand. Even the bright green and blue ones don't draw too much attention. Every time you catch yourself saying something negative to yourself (along the lines of the examples on page 112), snap your elastic HARD. Then say something positive to yourself. I learned this technique from the book *The One Minute Millionaire: The Enlightened Way to Wealth* by Robert G. Allen and Mark Victor Hansen (Crown Publishing Group, 2009). Keep the elastic on all the time. You never know when that nasty negative voice will try and catch you off guard, even once you have trained yourself not to listen to it. Be sure to wear your elastic band in the shower. There is a lot of time to think when you are showering!
2. Anytime you think a negative thought, go to the mirror, take a deep, cleansing breath, and say something positive to yourself instead. Don't forget to smile at yourself! Just let the negative

thought go. Don't give it a second thought. Don't let it have that kind of power over you. Your mind can only consciously think of one thought at a time. Increase the amount of time that there is a positive one in there.

3. In the *Tools To Life* program (toolstolife.com), Coach Devlyn Steele teaches you to assess the things you say to yourself. In the case that there may be some truth to the negative things you are saying about yourself, accept it and commit to moving on. After all, you *can* change! You have the power. If the things you say to yourself are not true, stop saying those things to yourself immediately. Do not lie to yourself anymore. That's really the least you can do. The most you can do is up to you.

4. If there is something in your life that you have done that you regret, you need to forgive yourself. Another effective tool that Coach Steele teaches is to write out the event on a piece of paper. Read it over, then go to the bathroom and rip the paper up into tiny little shreds and flush it down the toilet. Time to move on. It was a lesson learned, but it does not need to define who you are for the rest of your life. Negatively talking to yourself can actually make you do more things that are negative. You are labeling yourself a "bad person" and by doing this, you are giving yourself permission to act out again. Make amends with yourself. Forgive yourself.

5. Turn the volume down on the negative voice and turn the volume up on the positive voice. This is another technique I learned from the authors of *The One Minute Millionaire*. Every time you have a negative thought, imagine that you are using a volume button to turn the voice down so low that you can no longer hear it. Now listen for that positive voice and turn it up! How do we identify that positive voice? It is just like a muscle. The more you use it, the bigger and stronger it gets.

6. Consider what you are being negative about, and why. Just thinking: "Oh, that was pretty negative!" helps you identify those thoughts and allows you to turn your problems into opportunities for learning and making positive changes in your life.

7. Write down all the good things about you: accomplishments, skills, traits and other qualities. Start to consider what your own personal "superpower" might be. In my case, I have a keen sense of smell (too good at times!) and I am amazing at remembering numbers. I have no fear. I'm also an ace at delegation and staying focused. Think I'm busy now and can't handle anything else? Bring it on! Just call me "Super Tina!" Write down your own incredible traits and focus on them. Don't worry about the things you do not do well. There are others out there that can handle those things. Instead, do the things that you are amazing at, and that you most enjoy. You do not have to do everything yourself.

8. Get a good support system in place. When you are feeling negative it is helpful to have someone in your life that can give you a boost of positivity and a little perspective. Happiness is internal, but it helps to have a little external help as well.

BE THAT GIRL

Prepare a surprise for someone in your life to show you care. Help someone without them asking and without the expectation of getting anything in return. Think about what you are going to do, plan it and then do it!

When it comes to reading horoscopes, I personally favor the Chinese horoscope, at least when it comes to personality traits. In my experience, the Chinese horoscope more accurately depicts my own traits and the traits I see in others. I can assure you I am *definitely* a dragon. When you read your horoscope, only take in the positive words, the content and phrases that make you feel great about yourself. Often we look to external sources like horoscopes to help us define or redefine ourselves, or tell us what is going to happen in our lives. The fact of the matter is that you have it all within you right now to define yourself as whatever you want to be. So, Be That Girl!

Accentuate the Positive: Be Energetic

We only have so much energy everyday. We can always generate more energy through yoga or meditation or exercise, but even so, our energy is not infinite. We need to be choosy about what we do with our lives and with whom. Negativity is an energy sucker. Do not allow others to "steal" your energy.

If you feel drained physically and emotionally after hanging out with someone, you need to stop giving them your energy and stop spending time with them. This is *your* life, after all. It's better to associate with people who are positive and full of energy and ideas. Hang out with people who light a fire in you and inspire you to be your best everyday. Look for people who are doing, or have done, the things you want to do in life.

Accentuate the Positive: Be Honest

Be honest with yourself and others at all times. You will build trust in yourself when you are honest with yourself, and others. This means you need to listen to yourself at all times. You know what is best for you, and you cannot let others pressure you into a thought or action that does not work for you. Listen to your intuition, and to your positive voice, and do not compromise. Sometimes, you may think you are going to hurt someone's feelings if you are honest with them. As an example, let's say that you have made plans with your best friend to go out for dinner. That evening, you are just not in the mood to go out. Rather than making up an excuse of why you cannot go (my kids are sick, I have too much work to do, etc.) just be honest and tell your friend the real situation. A true friend will always understand where you are coming from and will not make you feel guilty (though they may tell you that they will miss you and that they were looking forward to hanging out with you). If you lie to your friends, it will always come back to bite you in the butt.

This also applies to recommending things to others. Only vouch for things that you really do believe in. This is especially true if you work in sales. Don't just try to sell something to someone that you know they won't need, or that doesn't actually work the way you say it will. You may make a sale in the short term, but you will lose the confidence of people in the future. Have integrity and do not compromise that for a quick buck. I always appreciate it when a server in a restaurant gives me an honest answer about what is good (or not good) on the menu, or when a clothing salesperson is truly honest about what looks good on me. When you lie, even if no one else knows, you will know that you lied. You will know that you were not honest. Your subconscious mind will accept that it is okay to lie to yourself and others, and from that point on, you will have a harder time being honest with yourself. Build qualities of faith, positivity and integrity in yourself by always speaking the truth.

Accentuate the Positive: Just Breathe

Always remind yourself to breathe. I find myself holding my breath at times. I'm not sure if this is just a holdover from my former smoking habit, or if it is just my innate reaction to stress. Whatever the reason, I can assure you that holding your breath is not good. When you are in pain, breathe through it. When you are frustrated, breathe through it. Take deeper and longer breaths whenever you can. It can be enlightening to focus on your breathing. We don't normally think about our breathing at all. It is an automatic bodily function that technically doesn't require any thought. But if you do focus on your breathing, you can use it to control your emotions and your body.

Take a minute to try this simple exercise:

> Find a quiet space and sit up tall. Roll your shoulders up and back and push them down (stick your chest out just a little); this will really increase the amount of space that your lungs have for breathing. Now close your eyes. Think only of your breathing and try to push away all other thoughts. Let any other thoughts that come into your head go, and focus on breathing through your nose. Breathe in through the nose for as long as you can, until your lungs feel nice and full. Pause for a second (hold your breath) before exhaling through your nose (no mouth breathing) as slowly as you can. Empty out your lungs as much as possible. Repeat this inhale-exhale cycle three times.

As you do these breathing exercises, focus on the space between the exhalation and inhalation. Think about that pause in your breath and the calm emptiness at that point. Focusing on something, instead of trying to focus on nothing, will help to keep other thoughts at bay. Each time you repeat a breath, try to increase the amount of time that you take to inhale and exhale. Don't rush. You are increasing the amount of oxygen in your body, and decreasing the stress, emotion and worry. Each inhalation will add strength, vitality, and calm. Each exhalation will reduce stress and cleanse your body and mind. Welcome to the world of meditation!

This simple exercise shouldn't take more than two minutes, and can be done anywhere, at any time. It will help you focus on the day ahead. Start with three breaths first thing in the morning and increase the amount of time you spend on this exercise when you feel ready. It will help you relieve anxiety and deal with pain, frustration and disappointment. It will also ground you and help you tap into the power of the Universe. The more you do this, the more you will think consciously about your breath, which will encourage you to take deeper, more cleansing breaths. Everyone has time for this easy exercise that can change your life — for the better.

Accentuate the Positive: Just Sing

The inspiration for this chapter ("*Ac-cent-tchu-ate the Positive*") is the title of a classic song. When you think about it, there is a song for every moment in life, so go ahead and sing it! Singing can make you feel so much better. Sing in the car. Sing in the shower. Sing while you're cleaning and cooking. Sing karaoke! Don't be embarrassed. Try it just once. If you hate it, then don't do it again. It's kind of like the "one-bite rule" I have for my kids: you may think you don't like a particular food, but you cannot actually make that decision until you try at least one bite. The same goes with karaoke, or anything else for that matter. How will you find out whether or not you like something if you are too afraid to try it?

Once you know that you do not like something, you don't have to do it again. And don't feel like it is a waste of time trying things that you end up not liking. This is what life is all about: learning what motivates us, learning what inspires us and what we are passionate about, and also learning what things to leave be. If you only do things that you are comfortable with, everything will stay exactly as it is. If you are satisfied with that, then change nothing. If you are excited to create some kind of change — any kind of change — then take action. Never stop trying new things. This will ensure that you are never bored. Always try something once!

Accentuate the Positive: Just Dance

Do not be afraid to dance in front of others. Music and motion can really ease tension and make you feel like a kid again. When you are feeling blue, turn on your favorite music and move around.

You will change the energy in yourself right away. Sometimes when my kids are driving me crazy (I am definitely *not* perfect, especially when it comes to being a mom of three independent-minded girls!) I turn the music on really loud and we have ourselves an impromptu dance party. Everyone ends up laughing and we all get a little exercise. When you are by yourself, crank the tunes and shake your booty. If you're in the car, crank your tunes and do some serious shimmying in your seat. Not only will you feel better but you're bound to get a smile out of the people in the cars around you. Get that positive energy oozing out of you. Sing, dance and be happy!

Accentuate the Positive: Keep Learning

One of my favorite movies of all time is *The Matrix* (yes, Ryan and I even named our first daughter "Trinity" after the character played by Carrie-Anne Moss). In *The Matrix*, if the characters needed to learn something they downloaded a computer program into their brains, and *voila!* — they could instantly become a helicopter pilot, or anything else they wanted! For us non-*Matrix* characters it might not happen quite that fast, but even so, remember that you have the ability to learn *anything*. Do not limit yourself. What have you always wanted to do, or be? Now is the time to look into what it would take to do it.

Eliminate the Negative: Tune Out

One easy way to "eliminate the negative" is to stop watching the news on TV, stop listening to the news on the radio and stop reading it in the newspaper. The news inundates us with negativity, so turn it off. How will you know what's happening? In his book *The 4-Hour Workweek* (Crown Archetype, 2009) author Timothy Ferriss suggests using your ignorance of the news as a conversation booster. You will be able to find out everything you need to know about the world by talking to others who are up to speed.

In addition to this, if you put the time that you are currently spending watching, listening or reading the news into doing something else like reading motivating books, working on a website or exercising, you will start seeing more results in your life. Focus on the things that will get you positive results, and tune out the negativity as much as possible.

Eliminate the Negative: Explore Your Anger

Anger is a secondary emotion. We feel angry because of some other emotion, like jealousy or sadness. Find out what the primary emotion is, and explore why you are feeling jealous or sad. Then change it. You can choose to feel content and happy. Take two minutes every day just to take in your surroundings and enjoy what is happening in your life. Enjoy those minutes, regardless of whether your day is stressful, exciting, dangerous, crazy, fun or calm. Your life is just a compilation of your experiences, so start really experiencing it by recognizing what your life is, and then enjoying it. Smile at what you have created and continue creating.

Eliminate the Negative: Can the "Can't"

Remove the word "can't" from your vocabulary. Instead of "can't," say you "choose not to" do something. "Can't" takes your power away and makes you feel that you have been defeated. If you "choose not to" do something, then you are in control and you have given yourself back the power to make decisions that work for you. Inspire confidence in yourself by always talking positively to yourself. Never say: "I'll never do that!" You'll eat your words at some point. Learn from everything you do and try not to judge yourself too harshly, but do give yourself high expectations and goals. Push yourself and challenge yourself. Laugh at yourself and those situations when you feel like you might cry. Take back your power and make the best of every situation.

Eliminate the Negative: Shield Yourself

I am a firm believer in the idea of the "invisible shield." I believe we can protect ourselves, and our families, by surrounding everyone with an invisible shield. I project this shield around myself, my children, my husband and our home at all times. It makes me feel protected and safe, and if I believe I am protected and safe, I will be. I always remind my children to have their invisible shields up, especially when they are feeling scared. My three-year-old likes to say to me: "I always have it on, Mom!" The invisible shield is especially comforting if you hate being alone in your home at night. Nothing can penetrate that invisible shield. Believe it and use it. Calm yourself and protect yourself. Once you have your shield on (and that should be all the time), you can stop thinking about all of the bad things that might happen to you. And once you stop thinking about those negative things, you will be even more protected against them.

Eliminate the Negative: Don't Worry

It was Bob Marley who famously sang: "*Don't worry, 'bout a thing, 'cause every little thing's gonna be alright.*" Wise words! Worrying is pointless.

Dwelling on things that might happen and that you have no control over is useless and negative behavior. The more you think about anything, the more likely it is to happen, so only think about positive, joyful, exciting things. "*But what if...*" you might be saying. Well, "*what if*" anything? Deal with things as they happen instead of always considering the "*what if.*" Obviously, you do need to prepare yourself for various outcomes to different situations (if you are waiting on the bank to approve a loan, for example, ensure you have thought about what your next action step will be depending on the bank's decision), but don't sit idly by and worry. Take action. If you are prepared for various outcomes and have an appropriate action plan, you should be able to put your worries aside. Worrying causes stress and it is not a productive way to manage your life. Don't worry. Make a plan, and take things as they come.

Eliminate the Negative: Watch what you say.

If you have nothing nice to say, don't say anything at all. Keep it to yourself. Negativity breeds negativity, and there is no need to pass your negative thoughts on to others. Journal your negative thoughts instead of sharing them and you will be able to work things out with yourself in a more positive way. Always share your joyful thoughts and feelings with others and curb your enthusiasm for sharing the nasty and negative. There will be times when you need to address issues with others. When this happens keep your emotions in check and always try to say things in a logical way. Do not take on other people's negativity. Remove yourself quickly from situations that are negative, or change the subject to something more constructive. Strive for positivity everyday, but don't be too hard on yourself when you fall back into your old habits. Just learn to recognize the pattern.

Now that you have some tactics under your belt to stay on the positivity train, let's take the happiness process a step further and learn how to "fake it 'til you make it!"

CHAPTER 12

Fake It 'Til You Make It

"Formulate and stamp indelibly on your mind
a mental picture of yourself as succeeding.
Hold this picture tenaciously. Never permit it to fade.
Your mind will seek to develop the picture...
Do not build up obstacles in your imagination."
– Norman Vincent Peale

Let's get down to the real nitty-gritty.

If you want to Be That Girl, you are going to have to learn how to "fake it 'til you make it." And you are going to have to become *unforgettable*. To do that, you're going to create a vision in your head of how you should look when you are successful.

Get out your pen and another piece of paper because you have some more work to do. Think about, and then answer the following questions:

How Do You Define Success?

(example answers)

- Success is making a lot of money.
- Success is having more time (for my family, for golfing, yoga, etc.).
- Success is being famous.
- Success is landing an amazing job.
- Success is no longer needing a job.
- Success is not feeling stressed out.

How Will You Know You Have Succeeded?

- I will have $1 million cash in the bank and no debt.
- I will have complete freedom and the time to do what I want, when I want. I will be golfing three times a week. I will do yoga every day for at least one hour.
- I will star in an A-list movie, I will have a No. 1 song on the charts, I will have a book on the *New York Times* Bestseller List, I will have paparazzi outside my house!
- I will be working at a company that respects me and I will enjoy going to work everyday.
- I will be making $(insert amount here), and I will be working less than 40 hours per week.
- I will wake up every day knowing I do not HAVE to go anywhere! I will not be controlled by a job.
- I will be calm and happy and never worried about money. I will handle things rationally and logically, and I will enjoy every day.

What Does A "Successful" Person Look Like In Your Head?

- Glamorous clothes and shoes.
- Well-dressed, put together.
- Great hair and beautiful skin.
- Someone who gets noticed and is unforgettable.

There are no correct answers to these questions and the ideas listed are merely there to get you thinking. You need to be honest with yourself about what you would like your success to look like. The important part of this exercise is to create a vision in your head of how YOU will look when you are successful. You should have that picture in your head now.

Take five minutes to meditate on this image. Sit on the floor in a cross-legged position. Sit up tall and place your hands palms up on your lap. Take five deep, cleansing breaths and then close your eyes. Picture yourself successful. You know now what you will look like, so focus on that. See That Girl, and you will Be That Girl.

The more clearly you can see That Girl in your head, the faster you will be able to manifest her. Quietly watch the successful girl in your head. See how she walks and how she is dressed. Feel what it is like to Be That Girl. Before you open your eyes, send out a huge thank you to the Universe for sending you what you need. Open your eyes and put your hands together in a prayer position in front of your chest and bow your head.

How do you feel after that exercise? Ready to take on the world? Calm and at peace? Never lose sight of that successful person. Stay focused on her at all times. Congratulate yourself! You have just tapped into the infinite Universe. This is one of the hardest steps, figuring out who you want to be and what you want your success to feel like. With that done, everything else is going to fall into place. I am so excited for you!

BE THAT GIRL

Never say "I can't do that," especially if you've never tried! Don't let fear hold you back. Don't hold yourself back.

"Faking it 'til you make it" means taking on tasks with vigor, even though you may not know much about what you are doing. When we purchased our first liquor store, I knew as much about wine as any average consumer and I sure as heck did not know much about owning and operating a retail store. But that did not stop me from pursuing this business opportunity. Instead of focusing on what I didn't know, I focused on how I would acquire the knowledge that I needed to be successful at this business. In our purchase agreement for the store, I added in one month of training by the previous owner, so that he could teach me all of the ins and outs of the business. I could tweak it to my own specifications after that, but I wanted to learn the basics and benefit from his knowledge of the industry.

Over the last five years, I have been a good girl and done my fair share of "homework" so that I could learn about wine. Who needs formal training when you can have real-world experience?

Learn just enough to get by and then get out there and figure out the rest by doing. Don't restrict yourself because of what you don't have or don't yet know.

It is important to remember that the concept of "fake it 'til you make it" doesn't mean you should be a fake person. The key is to have aspirations without sacrificing your own authenticity. If you are putting on airs, you will eventually get caught "not being you."

It is important to trust yourself and have others trust you. Be yourself and you will not fail yourself or others. Embrace your uniqueness. We are all different, and that is a great thing. Imitate others when it benefits you, but do it in a way that you still maintain your special individuality. If you love your quirks and use them to your advantage, you will find you don't care so much about what others think of you, and others will start recognizing you for those amazing differences.

People who take issue with your differences are either jealous of you and want to be like you, or they are just spiteful. Either way, the only opinion you should care about is your own. If you feel amazing, you will be amazing. Never doubt your own instincts. You know deep down in your gut what is right.

How you present yourself to the world will have a huge impact on the results you get. It's time to make sure you are dressed to kill.

CHAPTER 13

Get Dressed For Success

"It isn't what I do, but how I do it.
It isn't what I say, but how I say it,
and how I look when I do it and say it."
– Mae West

My husband always tells me that as women, we dress for other women. We look at other women all the time and judge them and ourselves. Men, for the most part, do not care whether or not you are wearing certain styles or brands. They care about the total package (you) and about making sure that "package" is happy (if that means lots of shoes, so be it!) With this in mind, decide just who it is you are dressing for.

When you get ready in the morning, do it with the intention of being able face anything that might come your way. You never know if and when you are going to meet that extraordinary contact who has the information you've been seeking, so you'd better be ready just in case. You do not want to be caught in your sweatpants (unless they are super-stylish lululemons) when you meet your next "millionaire mentor," so give yourself ample time each morning to get ready. Maybe that means showering in the evening. However you do it, figure out how to get your butt in gear early enough to be able to create a look that makes a lasting impression.

Hair

Your appearance shapes the way you feel about yourself. How do you feel right now? Let's start with your hair. Are you happy with your hair? Does your haircut make you feel powerful and sexy and beautiful? If you don't immediately reply "Yes!" then it is time for a change.

If you have been seeing the same hairdresser for years and you are not crazy-excited about your hair, you need to find a new hairdresser who will be open to giving you a new look. Do not be afraid to do this. Change is good. There is always an amazing haircut that will suit your personality, your time constraints and your beauty skills. Let's face it, we only have so much time to allocate to doing our hair and some of us could not use a curling iron if our lives depended on it. An amazing hairdresser will give you not just a great hairstyle but one that fits into your lifestyle as well. Good, honest communication with your hairdresser is so important. If you are not feeling the love, then move on. It's nothing personal.

I used to revel in having long, straight hair that I could put in braids, buns and ponytails. A good friend of mine, who happens to be a hairdresser, said to me one day: "you know, you could be so gorgeous if you would just do something with your hair!"

At first, I was mortally offended! But sometimes the truth hurts and this was information that I truly needed to bring out my inner glamour girl. Another friend had a cute angled bob and eventually I got up the courage to try a similar look. It was truly life changing. I have not looked back since! I was never a "girly girl" before but the new haircut made me feel sexy, gorgeous, sassy and successful, and now that I am more confident in my cut, I have started to play with different colors, just to keep things interesting. So take it from someone who knows: having great hair will change the way you feel about yourself immediately. Embrace the change.

Skin

Now how about that gorgeous face of yours, are you happy with the tone of your skin? If not, you need to take steps to get your skin where you want it. Rather than using makeup to cover up skin issues, focus on fixing the problem and clearing up your skin. There are a lot of great, natural products out there these days, so start sampling some of them. I personally like the Dr. Hauschka line, but everyone is different and you need to find something that your skin likes. The better your skin is, the less makeup you will feel you need to use and the better you will feel about yourself.

When it comes to makeup, I prefer to accentuate my natural features rather than look like I'm wearing lots of makeup. I use eyeliner and mascara to make my eyes look larger and a little bit of bronzing powder to give me a healthy glow. If I'm feeling really special, I put on colored lip gloss. For me, less is more. Too much makeup is just another form of clutter in your life! Imagine how nice your makeup cupboard would look if you only had a couple of items. You do not need a lot of makeup. You are beautiful just the way you are.

Nails

Now let's talk nails. Start making regular visits to your local "splash 'n' dash" nail salon. These are places that specialize in good-value manicures and pedicures in a clean environment. Manicures and pedicures do cost money but they make you feel like a million bucks. Sorry to say, but most feet are unattractive, so scrubbing and prettying up those toenails can really change the way you feel. Find a way to budget for this, or, if money is tight, take care of it yourself at home. Having nicely manicured fingernails will even make you type differently. Just watch!

Unwanted Hair

A good salon will also offer waxing or threading services to remove unwanted facial hair. Getting your eyebrows shaped and removing dark upper-lip hair will have a huge impact on how you feel about yourself. The specialists at the salon will be able to recommend what you need to have done as far as hair removal on your face. Take their advice!

Do not leave this up to your friends. They will withhold the truth from you when it comes to your looks because they love you and want to protect your feelings. Your salon or spa professional will always give an objective opinion as to what you need, so take their advice, and, more importantly, feel great about it. Take steps to remove the hair from your legs, armpits and bikini area often enough that you will be ready for anything. Shaving is the cheapest option, but it needs to be done frequently. Waxing is more expensive, but it does last longer than shaving. It can also be painful and time consuming. I will not discuss depilatory creams as just the smell of these could remove your nose hairs. That cannot be good for you!

Being of Hungarian and French Canadian descent, I was "blessed" with a lot of dark body hair. When I relied on shaving, I would do it in the morning and end up having stubble by the evening. Laser hair removal is by far my favorite method. It is quite expensive at the outset, however, after a few treatments, you will be mostly hair free. Even if you can only afford one or two treatments, it will noticeably cut down on the amount of hair that grows back. It is still a painful option, but it takes less time than waxing and is less messy.

With waxing, when you leave the salon your legs will be nice and smooth. With laser hair removal your legs will smell like burnt hair and most of the hair will still be there — even though the laser has killed the hair follicle, it takes several days for the hairs to fall out on their own. So do not expect to leave your laser session hair free! Whatever option you choose, removing the hair from your legs, armpits, bikini line (go for a full "Brazilian" if you are daring!) makes you feel smooth and sexy, to yourself and others.

Clothes

Now you need to put that gorgeous body into some gorgeous clothes. What you wear says a lot about you. Do you usually throw on jogging pants and a ball cap to go grocery shopping? Even on simple errands, your clothing should be a reflection of your personal style and should also reflect your "status." First impressions can make it or break it. Notice how amazing you feel when you put on a new outfit that fits you to a T and is a flattering color and style for you. When you wear clothes that you like and that make your body look good, you feel good on the inside too, powerful and confident. You will walk taller and prouder when you are wearing your favorite clothes. Your vision of yourself improves when you wear items that hug all the right curves and that vision is transmitted to everyone around you. People cannot help but be drawn to you when you are exuding this positive energy. That's why you need to dress this way everyday.

I want you to consider what you are saying to other people by the clothes you wear on a regular basis. Do your clothes have holes, rips or loose threads? Sure they may be your favorite clothes, but what message are you sending? "I am not confident," "I cannot afford other clothes," "I do not care about my appearance," "I do not care enough about myself." As a society, we have adopted the saying: "Don't judge a book by its cover." Yet, the subconscious mind takes in everything and judgments are formed based on observations. This happens within seconds of a stimulus being introduced and it applies to yourself and others. You *will* be judged on your appearance. That's not to say you need to care about everyone's opinions. As my dad says: "Opinions are like assholes; everybody has one and they usually stink."

The person that you should care most about impressing is you, but since you never know when you are going to run into an important contact, you have got to be ready to give the right impression. You will do this if you truly believe in yourself. So start dressing the part. Remember the vision of "successful you" from Chapter 12: Fake It 'Til You Make It? That is your style model. Be That Girl. Act like her, dress like her, do the things she would do. Convince yourself that you are That Girl and you will be her.

Lingerie

When it comes to clothing, money is an issue for most of us. After all, if you could afford to be wearing all the clothes that you wanted, wouldn't you be doing it already? First things first. Some of your clothing budget should be spent on a few good bras and matching panties. Good-quality bras that are sexy and pretty and fit well are one of the best investments you can make. Once you have them, if you wash them properly in cold water and hang them to dry, they will last for years and years.

Putting on a pretty bra that keeps the "girls" in their proper upright position, and then putting on a pair of pretty matching panties will make you feel like a goddess every day. Your subconscious will know you are wearing these items and you will walk differently. Trust me on this! If you are well endowed, it is even more important to get a well-fitted bra. Most specialty lingerie stores will be happy to fit you. The items at specialty lingerie stores will also be much more expensive but do not feel that you have to buy anything there, just consider it research. Get fitted, try on a couple amazing bras, check out the prices and then confidently walk out of there, but not before taking note of some of the brand names that you tried on and liked. You can then go home and search online for these brands. Check out other styles on the brand websites and compare online prices at other stores.

Being a little small in this department, I have always had a difficult time finding bras (I think finding the right bra is difficult for everyone!) But I eventually discovered a brand with just the right amount of foam, comfort and sexiness at a local lingerie boutique. I ended up buying one bra there and then went home and searched for that same brand online. Turns out most major department stores in my city also carry this line of bras. Of course, the level of service at a small boutique is far better than the department store, which is why they can justify charging more.

Although I am all for supporting independent boutiques, at the end of the day, I am a girl on a budget. So if, like me, you know what you are looking for, you can then go and save money by buying lingerie at department stores. Your goal should be to find at least five bras that fit you well and make you feel pretty. Make sure you have one white, one black and one natural or cream-colored bra. The other two can be as fun and flirty as you want. You may also want to invest in a good strapless bra.

Don't forget the matching panties, or panties that will go nicely with your bra styles. Remember that these items are investments in you. They are going to cost money but this is one area where you should not scrimp. Quality is the most important thing to consider, so if you are looking to save a few dollars, hold out for sales or "scratch-and-save" days. Try to replenish your lingerie wardrobe by buying one new bra each year.

Pretty bras and matching panties will make you feel like a goddess even before you put your clothes on. These little items are an investment in you, so be sure you "hang-to-dry" your lingerie so it lasts.

Bras and panties are great for making you feel good in the daytime, but they can also double as nighttime ammunition. Want to impress your man? All you need is a pair of high-heeled shoes and a sexy bra with matching panties. Shoes worn in the bedroom will instantly transform your daytime garb into sexy nighttime lingerie.

You won't have to spend any more money on fancy lingerie to impress your man. This is truly all you need to spice things up (although it certainly doesn't hurt to add thigh-high, stay-up sexy stockings).

Now for the rest of your clothes. It really does not matter what is "in style." Let your own style out. Wear what you feel comfortable in and what makes you feel good, while still dressing like the "successful you." It really does not matter if you are thin as a rail, or if you have a little extra padding. If you wear clothes that compliment your curves, or your slimness you are sending out the message that you are amazing. People will not be looking at your clothes. They will be looking at the beautiful package that is you and thinking: "Damn, she looks fine!"

Looking Good On A Budget

Until you have that extra $1,000 to spend on clothes every week, you've got to spend what you do have smartly. A good way to do this is to start shopping at consignment and secondhand stores. There are many different kinds of secondhand stores. Some specialize in high-end designer fashions, while others will accept anything. Do a little online searching to find out what is around you, and then do a little reconnaissance mission to the ones that sound promising. Figure out how they price their clothes and what day of the week they put out their new stock, then plan to go back on that day so that you will have first pickings of all the new stuff. Some secondhand stores have half-price days each month, so be sure to ask the staff about those sorts of events. Be prepared to spend some time secondhand shopping, as you will have to search through lots of things to find the right pieces.

I personally like to shop at Goodwill for a number of reasons. You certainly can't beat the prices, plus the proceeds go to charity. They also have great stock. I frequently find brand-name items in great condition for $6.99 or less!

Get yourself a few new outfits that fit you well and are appropriate for the "successful you" to wear. Secondhand stores also carry shoes, accessories and purses.

You will be amazed at the brands of shoes you can find there. Plus, they will already be broken in! Take them home and wash them well. If the thought of wearing used clothes makes you squeamish, you need to get over it. Change your thinking. Instead of worrying about wearing someone else's old clothes, start being thankful that they decided to give it away so you could be wearing it at a fraction of the price!

Another secondhand shopping tip is to check the clothes for rips, tears, missing buttons, stains or general wear and tear. If there is a button missing and you still absolutely love the item, ask for a discount and then take it to a tailor to sew on a new button. Or, if you are eager, stop at a sewing store, pick up a new button and sew it on yourself. In the end, this will still be less expensive than buying the item new.

I get compliments on my clothes all of the time, and the majority of what I wear is secondhand. It is all about how you wear the clothes that makes them look great. The same clothes always look different on someone else. Secondhand stores don't just stock current clothing trends, allowing you to explore your own personal style without outside influences. Try not to be controlled by the fashion-marketing machine and choose your clothes based on what you like and what looks good on you. It's good if we don't all look exactly the same. Express yourself and you will get yourself noticed.

Shoes

Shoes are the ultimate accessory. A pair of beautiful shoes changes an entire outfit and it changes your mindset too. How many pairs do you need? One pair for every outfit seems about right! Plus, a few extra pairs bought with the intention of finding an outfit to go with them later on. What I'm saying here is have fun buying shoes. They can be expensive but they can also make or break an outfit.

Fashion aside, the most important thing about your shoes is that they are clean and scruff-free. When I worked at Safeway, the head cashier told me the first thing she looks at during interviews is what the applicant was wearing on their feet. Were their shoes clean and appropriate, or grungy and scuffed? It's a good reminder that people are making judgments about you all the time, so give them the right impression. Again, it is not about having the right brand names. No one will ever know how much you paid, or what brand your shoes are, unless you tell them. Pick shoes that are classy, pretty and match your outfits.

Comfort is important, but let's face it, most high-heeled shoes are not comfortable. It's the price of beauty, ladies! The best advice I can give you on comfort is to break your shoes in well before wearing them. Strut around the house in your heels for practice. If your shoes are so uncomfortable that you cannot keep them on for more than five minutes, then they are not the right shoes. But if you can wear them for two-to-three hours before they start making your feet hurt, they are probably great shoes.

I have noticed that the more expensive the shoes are, the longer they last and, generally, the more comfortable they are (justify your shoe spending however you like, but do not blame it on me!).

If you are on a budget, buy a couple pairs of shoes that are versatile and can be worn with most of your outfits. Try second-hand stores, or just buy cheaper shoes in the meantime. Once the money is rolling in, you can add more, and more, and more pairs of shoes. *To infinity… and beyond!*

Accessories

Less is more when it comes to accessorizing. The rule here should be to accentuate your outfit, not take attention away from it.

Draw people's eyes to a gorgeous necklace, or a nice pair of earrings, but do not clutter yourself with accessories. When you wear too many accessories, people will not know where to look because there is so much going on. Do not hide behind your accessories and jewelry. Choose wisely and wear one or two items. Hats can really get you some attention. I truly believe that there is a hat for everyone, so those of you who are saying: "I can't wear hats," have not yet found the right hat. The right hat will make you feel powerful and interesting. You will know it is the right hat by the way it makes you feel when you put it on.

Purses

Though I love purses, they're not as much of an obsession for me as shoes. For me, a purse needs to be functional and cute. That said, some women totally judge each other on the brand of their satchel. If you are concerned about the brand of your purse, and are on a tight budget, check out secondhand stores, or buy a fake (fake it 'til you make it, right?) No one will know the difference except you. If someone does know it's a fake, the reality of the situation is that purse still looks great on you. It is all about how you feel that matters: you, you, you! This is the first and foremost opinion you should care about.

No matter what purse you are using, make sure you keep it clean and tidy, just like your home. Be sure to empty your purse of gum wrappers, receipts and anything else you don't need. The less you keep in your purse, the better your back and shoulders will feel and the easier it will be to find the things you need when you need them. For those of you who are purse swappers and change up your purses daily, buy a small cosmetic bag for all the things that you regularly swap out: chapstick, lipstick, personal monthly items, nail file, Band-Aids, allergy pills, business cards, etc.

This will make it easier to swap purses without leaving behind something important. Promote good energy surrounding your money by getting a red wallet. According to the principles of Feng Shui, the color red will help to multiply your wealth.

As they say in the musical *Annie*: "You're never fully dressed without a smile," so start your day off right by smiling at yourself in the mirror. You deserve to feel happy first thing in the morning, and the first person you should smile at is you! If you start with a smile, you will have a better chance of keeping that smile and that happiness with you all day long. Dress yourself with a smile everyday!

CHAPTER 14

Walk the Walk

"For beautiful eyes, look for the good in others;
for beautiful lips, speak only words of kindness;
and for poise, walk with the knowledge
that you are never alone."
– Audrey Hepburn

Now that you are dressed for success, you need to start walking the walk. How you present yourself in this way will have a direct impact on what you can accomplish everyday.

Some of us may remember our parents saying: "Sit up straight! Don't slouch!" And our response being something like: "Yeah, whatever mom! Gosh, you're always telling me what to do!" Looking back, I am grateful that my parents stressed the importance of good posture and a proud stature. This was something that was reinforced when I began practicing yoga. Focusing on standing straight and tall is extremely important — in yoga and in life.

Look around and you will notice two types of people: those who are confident in themselves and those who are not. How do you judge who is confident and successful and who is not? This is my take on the situation:

Successful people walk with confidence in every step. They keep their heads up and make eye contact. They are not worried about themselves, instead, they are constantly observing and watching, waiting for opportunities to be presented or lessons to be learned. They appear focused and determined and put-together, and they usually have a smile waiting for those who pass them by.

Someone who isn't confident will avoid eye contact at all costs. Their body language says it all — they slouch, look down most of the time and they may shuffle their feet instead of walking with nice, firm steps. It may be harder to elicit a smile out of someone who is not confident.

Even if you do not feel confident in yourself today, you should want others to *perceive* that you are confident. Start with walking tall and sitting tall. Walking the walk is extremely important if you are going to Be That Girl, and if you believe it, you will easily transmit that confident identity to others.

For those of you who have never had the pleasure of uttering "*ohmmmmmm*..." here is another yoga-inspired technique that you can bring into your everyday life. In yoga, a major focus is on elongating the spine. Having a nice, straight spine makes your body stronger and more flexible. All the signals that are transmitted from your brain to the rest of your body, and vice versa, travel through the spine. When the spine is straight, the signals are transmitted faster and with more precision. So not only are you going to work on your confidence here, you are also going to work on getting your body healthier too. Fellow yoga goddesses will be familiar with the following technique from their practice, but perhaps have never considered using it in during the course of daily life. Let's get started:

If you are standing, ground your feet into the floor. To ground literally means to put attention and focus into your feet and really feel the ground beneath you. Stabilize yourself with your feet as a

In mountain pose, you are strong, focused, and straight. Solid as a rock and confident in your space!

large tree would with its roots. Engage the muscles in your legs so they are firm and stable. Tuck your pelvis, squeeze your buttocks and engage your tummy muscles. This will get your spine in a proper alignment. Always keep your tummy muscles tight if you can.

Consciously thinking about squeezing those abs will do wonders for protecting your back and trimming your waistline. Now, roll your shoulders up, back and down, and keep them there. It will feel like you are squeezing your shoulder blades together in the back.

Your arms should be poised at your sides. Now keep your head up by elongating your neck and tilting your chin up slightly. Focus your eyes straight ahead as if you were looking at something amazing. Now stay like that for a few breaths and remember what it feels like. In yoga, this is called "Mountain Pose" and it is a very powerful way to focus your energy and refuel your body with energy from the Universe.

How does that feel? You should be feeling powerful, strong, stable and maybe just a bit strange. Remember that doing anything different will always feel weird at first, but as you practice more and more, it will eventually become a part of you and feel more natural.

For now, I want you consciously to think, "be a mountain," every time you are sitting, standing or walking. This will keep you tall, stable, grounded and focused. In the beginning, it will take a few seconds to stabilize yourself, roll your shoulders and get poised. But over time, you will only need to think "mountain!" and you will be in a ready position instantly. It will become a habit if you just keep at it.

Now, about how to walk... or "strut". I recently took a "Burlesquercise" class with my friend Annie. This was an exercise class cleverly disguised as "fun" by adding a burlesque element. Apart from yoga, I am not usually one for exercise classes, but I really did enjoy this one, even though it thoroughly kicked my butt! My tight abs made all that pain worth it. Anyways, one of the coolest things they taught in this class was how to "strut."

Why walk, when you can strut your way through life? Here's how:

Preparing to strut means getting your head in the game. Prepare to amaze!

Start your strut with whichever leg you were bending. Don't forget to step a bit into the middle. This gets that great hip action that everyone notices!

Maintain your confident smile, your posture, and your focus while you strut. You'll get more attention and you'll start seeing other things more clearly from your engaged and focused standpoint.

Starting from your stable "mountain" stance, place your left hand on your left hip, gently bend your left knee and lift your left heel so you are on your toes on your left foot. Put most of your weight on your right foot. Feels kind of sexy, right? Now think about something, or someone, that makes you smile and enjoy that sassy feeling. Lift up your left leg, point your toes and step forward, straight forward, not to the side. Then lift up your right leg and step straight in front of your left leg. Think of stepping forward, but directed toward the center. If you are moving your left leg, it will feel like you are stepping a bit to the right instead of in line with your leg, and vice versa with the right leg.

Move your hips as you walk and let your arms swing naturally. Keep thinking about being a mountain and maintain your tall position: shoulders back, chin up, tight tummy and buttocks. Keep your head up and scan your surroundings with your eyes. Always be aware of your surroundings. You never know when an opportunity is going to turn up and you need to be ready.

How do you feel when you strut? You should feel powerful, sexy and confident if you are doing it properly!

While you are walking the walk, don't forget that gorgeous smile. I like to walk around with what some might call a "Mona Lisa smile." Walking around with a huge toothy grin on your face will get you noticed all right, but maybe not for the right reasons, so I would recommend a soft, close-lipped smile for everyday outings. You might want to call this your "mysterious smile." It will appear to others that you have something amazing up your sleeve and of course, they will be intrigued to find out what your secret is. Of course, you know what it is: you are That Girl!

At this point, you should be feeling excited to try out the Be That Girl techniques. Remember, everything you are learning is designed to convince you that you are That Girl. Thinking it turns it into reality.

Now let's delve deeper and explore how you can garner strength and confidence from your personal connections.

CHAPTER 15

The Power of Touch

"We can live without religion and meditation,
but we cannot survive without human affection."
– The Dalai Lama

I learned a cute little song when my oldest daughter was in kindergarten. Her class sang it at the school's annual Mother's Day tea (my daughter was well represented by a huge group of grandmas, sisters and aunties; our family took up a whole table!). It goes something like this:

Four hugs a day, that's the minimum,
Four hugs a day, not the maximum...

Out of all the songs we heard that day, "Four Hugs a Day" really stuck with me. I found myself singing it a lot, and for good reason: hugging and other types of human contact is something that everyone needs.

If you cannot fulfill your "four hugs a day" quota, make sure you get at least one really good hug. Make that hug last as long as you can and enjoy the amazing feeling of being embraced in someone else's arms. A hug can make you feel supported, loved, cared for and important.

Hugging will make some people feel uncomfortable, but that's because it makes them *feel*. Hugging brings emotions to the surface. If you are having a rather hard day, and someone gives you a hug, that hug can start the tears flowing. Having emotions is not a bad thing. Putting your emotions out in the open, even for others to see them, is a healthy and normal part of life. Once the emotions are out there you can better recognize and deal with them. If they stay hidden, your mind will fixate on them and those emotions will build up over time, gathering weight like a snowball.

The ball will continue to get larger and larger until it grows too large to hide anymore and, eventually, you *will* be forced to deal with it.

As a society, we place value on being strong and unemotional, but that's not necessarily the best way to operate. You have got to let yourself cry when you need to cry. Don't worry about what other people will say or if they will judge you. It does not matter if someone sees you with red, puffy eyes. Of course, crying, and red, puffy eyes are likely to elicit concern in the form of: "Are you okay?" or "What's wrong?"

BE THAT GIRL

Chart your menstrual cycle on a calendar so you can plan for the inevitable. Just mark the first day with a circle around the date. Figure out your personal monthly schedule and make plans accordingly.

Most of the time, we will not want to discuss what is wrong — that's why we try to hide the fact that we are crying, or try not to cry at all. In that case, it's perfectly alright to reply with something along the lines of: "Actually, I don't want to talk about it right now, but thanks so much for asking. Perhaps you could tell me a funny story or a joke to cheer me up?" If you do, in fact, want to talk about it, then that's fine too. Either way, get the emotion out and then let go of it. Smile, even when you don't want to and turn the negative energy into positive energy.

Speaking of positive energy is there anything more positive than a good old "high five?" When someone does something cool or exciting, go up high! Positive human interaction doesn't have to be all about hugging. A solid high five is a great way to harness all that positive energy between you and someone else and celebrate it in one big happy burst. According to my sister Brenda, the secret to a great high-five is to focus on the other person's elbow. Do that and you'll never miss!

There is another kind of human touch that I'm going to discuss now, because it's important if you are going to Be That Girl. You are never too old, or too young, to start loving yourself and by that I mean loving yourself, and pleasuring yourself physically. After all, how can you expect to be pleasured by someone else if you do not feel comfortable enough to do it for yourself?

Having a healthy sexual relationship is all about communication — the right kind of communication. And since you are learning to be more confident in yourself all around, this crucial part cannot be pushed to the side.

There is a definite stigma about pleasuring yourself, especially for women. Some women have tried it as girls and loved it, but then forced themselves to stop for one reason or another. Any reasons you had for stopping, or never starting in the first place, are not important. What is important is that you overcome whatever fears you have and let down any walls you may have about this being inappropriate. You are a sexual being and you were designed to feel pleasure, and having a healthy sex life is an important component of any relationship. The more confidence you have in yourself in this area, the more likely you are to have confidence when you are with someone else.

I'm assuming that after reading Chapter 13: Get Dressed For Success, you are now smooth, sexy and wearing cute undies and pretty bras. You are sexy and it's a good thing! Embrace this feeling. Do not be afraid of fantasizing. It does not make you a bad person if you happen to think of someone other than your partner. It is healthy to fantasize, and it will really get the engine heating up.

Contrary to some beliefs, loving and satisfying yourself will not curb your desire to have sex — if anything it will make you want sex more often! Vibrators and toys can be fun to play around with, but you don't need to use them unless you want to (consider booking a "Passion Party" with a group of friends — these are basically X-rated versions of the classic "Tupperware Party" and they can be a lot of fun with just the girls, or with other couples).

Toys or no toys, you already have everything you need for this exercise. Find a place where you can relax, be comfortable and release some of the tension in your life. In my opinion, there is not too much in this world that a hot shower or bath can't cure. Get comfortable before you start fantasizing. Do not allow yourself to feel guilty; your fantasies are just thoughts and are being used here as tools for your success, not action items. If it makes you feel better, pick a famous person as your fantasy partner. The chances of anything happening for real with this person are slim to none, unlike a real person you might encounter in the course of daily life. Whenever it feels right for you, touch yourself lovingly. Start by giving yourself a nice arm rub, and then go from there.

Often for us women, if we are not "in the mood" there is really no way for us to be stimulated. It seems unfair that men are more likely to be in the "ready position," even if they are stressed out. For us girls, it may take a lot more effort. In the same way that stress can inhibit our libidos, men see sex as a stress reliever.

While we women are thinking about all the things we need to get done the next day, our men are quietly having dirty thoughts about Angelina Jolie. Well, I say two can play at that game. We need to change our thinking, ladies! The next time you are stressing out over when you're going to find the time to get groceries, try thinking about shirtless Brad Pitt wearing a pair of fireman coveralls and see what that does to your state of mind!

In any case, to start having amazing sex we need to take control over our sex lives. Sex is good for the body and the soul. Sex is also good for the mind. Having more sex with your partner will make you feel more relaxed, vibrant and better about yourself all around. Human touch is vital to our existence, so what better way to stay healthy than to be as close to someone as possible? Enjoy this process. It is meant to be fun and to feel good.

If you think you are not having enough sex (or your partner thinks it's not enough), do something about it. Change yourself, change your thinking or learn to communicate your needs better to your partner. Be prepared to give directions or helpful hints to

Sometimes a little romance can go a long way. Romance adds fuel to the fire of any relationship. The more effort you and your partner put into your love life, the more rewards you both get.

your partner whenever possible. This should not make them feel that they are not doing a good job, rather they will appreciate that you are helping them perfect the art of pleasing you. If this is their ultimate goal, they will be very grateful that you gave them guidance (and if it is not, perhaps it is time to find a partner who will make this a priority). Now that you know what you like (and what you don't like), you should have the confidence to make corrections and adjustments tactfully, and embrace all the pleasure you deserve.

Human contact is vital to a successful and happy life. Allow yourself to enjoy physical contact. Be comfortable with your body and allow yourself to be open to exploring the opportunities that others give you. It doesn't always have to be physical. Keeping yourself open and receptive to meeting new people and always being on the lookout for new opportunities will give you a leg up in all aspects of your life. Let's explore that further.

CHAPTER 16

Taking on the World

"It had long since come to my attention that people of accomplishment rarely sat back and let things happen to them. They went out and happened to things."
– Leonardo da Vinci

Okay you sexy goddess, now we need to work on getting you noticed outside the bedroom too! First of all, if you are going to Be That Girl, you are going to have to get used to getting more attention. This is not something to be scared of; it's a good thing! Trust me. You are done with being afraid, right? If you've got it, flaunt it. And you have it. Of course you do!

To get noticed, you need to do more noticing. This begins with the eyes. Making eye contact with others should not be confused with outright staring. When you are driving in your car and stop at a red light, turn your head to the left and to the right. If there is someone in the car beside you, make eye contact with them and smile, then turn your head straight again fairly quickly, before they get the misguided idea that you are trying to get their attention. Most people are so self-conscious, they cannot imagine looking over at someone beside them when they are in their car, so you may not always have a chance to make eye contact. You, on the other hand, are not that self-conscious person, so do this every time you are stopped at a light. The first time might seem weird, but each time after that will feel better and better.

When you do make eye contact with someone and smile, feel good knowing you have just helped that person. When someone smiles at you, it's very hard not to smile back. Just try *not* smiling when someone smiles at you, and you will see just how much effort that takes (you have to be pretty grumpy for it to be easy).

Returning a smile is easier than not returning a smile, so just think that every time you smile at someone you are making that person smile too. What an easy way to brighten someone's day!

Make eye contact with everyone you encounter. When you are at the supermarket, don't hide behind your grocery list. Look around at people, make eye contact and smile at others whenever you catch their eye. When you ask for lunchmeat at the deli counter, make eye contact with the person helping you, smile at them and ask them a question about their day. When you are in an elevator with someone else, don't just keep your head down and hope the other person doesn't notice you. You are not that kind of girl anymore! Keep your head up, make eye contact and smile at the other passengers. Once you get comfortable with eye contact and smiling, be courageous enough to initiate actual conversations with people. You might simply mention something that is relevant to the situation at hand, or you could comment on the weather, or something interesting that is happening in the world.

One of my favorite things to do is compliment people. Since I am always focused on my environment, I notice a lot of little things. As you are gazing around at your surroundings, do a once over on the people you see. Just try not to go overboard. Women need to be careful in this regard, especially if the other person is a man. Find something about that person that you can comment on, like their haircut or hair color, shoes, purse, clothes, nails, jewelry, kids, pet, etc. If you are at the supermarket, you might want to comment on something in their shopping cart (if you are so bold), or if you're at the park you might notice a book they are reading.

Just starting up a conversation with someone will help you pass the time in a lineup or elevator and make the experience more enjoyable. As always, you need to be conscious of the fact that there are no coincidences in life.

The people that you just "happen" to meet in a lineup, or elevator, or anywhere else for that matter, may have information for you, or you may have information for them. Be confident enough to seek out the information that is being laid out right in front of you and be willing to educate others. Help people and you will help yourself. Ask curious questions and start reveling in the answers you get.

When you are talking with someone, there are a few simple rules you can follow that can help you be an amazing conversationalist. First, always maintain eye contact. This ensures that the person you are conversing with knows you are interested in what they have to say. Be selfish, and always be listening for information that others have that can help you. If you are trying to gather information at all times, it will make you a very good listener and people will enjoy talking to you, which will help you gain more and more information. At the same time, always consider whether you have information in your head that you can give to this person, based on the things they are telling you. Do you know something valuable that they are hoping to learn? Be a giver and a taker when it comes to conversing, and you will be amazed at how exciting it can be.

This brings me to another point. When you do meet someone for the first time, you can use these rules to make the meeting as effective as possible.

Offer your hand to shake and ensure that handshake is firm.

A firm handshake means you grip the other person's hand snuggly but not too tightly. Keep your arm firm also. While you are shaking their hand, look directly into their eyes the entire time. The handshake should last only a few seconds, but it should be enough time to exchange names:

"Hi, I'm Tina."
"I'm Bridget."

It is extremely important to remember names. As this exchange happens so quickly, you must also be very quick.

When the person you meet says their name, make sure you hear it. If you did not, then immediately say: "Sorry, I didn't catch your name." Be sure to say that right away. As soon as they say their name, try and associate their name with something familiar in your life. Repeat their name in your head, and then associate it, quickly. I cannot stress this enough. You will eventually get better at this, but it does take practice. For example, if your new contact says: "I'm Bridget," in your head think: "Bridget, like *Bridget Jones' Diary*" or "Bridget, like my cousin," or "Bridget, like my old math tutor." If you've never heard their name before, or it is something uncommon such as "Anskin," repeat it in your head three times. Think: "Anskin, Anskin, Anskin."

Next, repeat their name back to them right away.

"So nice to meet you, Bridget."
"What an interesting name you have, Anskin."

Your next move is to use their name back to them two more times. The goal is to say their name three times within the first few minutes of meeting them.

Always ask people questions about themselves. People love to talk about themselves and this is a valuable way to start a conversation and figure out more about how that person can help you. I love to start with the question: "What do you do to fill your time?"

This avoids the whole: "What do you do for a living?" question, which may offend a stay-at-home mom, student or someone who is currently out of work. Finding out what someone does with their time will tell you all about them, what their skill sets are, what their hobbies might be and whether or not they have a family.

You can learn a lot from that question alone. It's also important to keep your questions pertinent to the particular situation you are in.

"Anskin, how did you get such an interesting name?

"Bridget, How long have you known (so-and-so)?"

"Anskin, I was wondering how long you have been involved in this field of study?"

Use the person's name as many times as you can right away, to help solidify it in your mind.

At this point, let's assume someone else has just walked into your conversation and they know you but they have not met "Bridget" or "Anskin." Now you really get to test your listening skills! Let's assume this person is Jessica, and you have known her for a while. You can now Be That Girl who introduces people and brings them together.

"Oh hi, Jessica. Bridget and I were just chatting about taking over the world! Jessica, this is Bridget. Bridget, this is Jessica. Jessica and I have known each other for two years. We have both been involved with this support group for about a year. Bridget owns her own flower shop and this is her first time at the support group."

Aren't you amazing? You are listening closely and retaining information. The biggest secret to remembering names (and anything else in life) is to tell yourself that you are amazing at it. Think of how you've spoken to yourself in the past in this regard. I'll bet it's something like:

"I'm terrible at remembering names! As soon as someone says their name, it is just gone!"

You need to understand that your subconscious hears everything you say and everything you think. Your subconscious then responds by doing exactly what you have told it. So if you continue to tell yourself that you are horrible with names, you will continue to be horrible at remembering names. This concept applies to everything you tell yourself. Start talking more positively to yourself and you will start seeing immediate changes. Remember that you can do anything you put your mind to, so start putting your mind to positive things. Take everything in so you don't miss a thing. The Universe is always putting things out there for you, but you need to be aware if you are going to see them.

The Art Of Effective Communication

Now that you know how to meet new people with ease and confidence, let's talk more about "the Big C" — by that I mean communication.

There are always a million things floating around in our heads. Your subconscious is inundated with thoughts all through the day and night. We listen to some and let the rest stay in the background.

As women, we need to be aware that no one can read our minds. Women tend to put way too much faith in the abilities of those around them to know exactly what they are thinking, and why. Sometimes, we want people to know what we are thinking.

"Didn't they just see how annoyed I got when
they didn't thank me for the dinner?"

"How can he not realize that I need help around the house? I
have been home all day with the kids... he knows
I need a break!"

"My friend can clearly see how annoyed I am
that she is making me drive again tonight
when she knows it is her turn."

"He knows how much it annoys me when
he leaves the toilet seat up!"

The truth is that no one instinctively knows how you feel, or why you feel that way. You are the only one that knows that. So you need to start taking responsibility and start sharing more. The only way you can expect things to change in your life is if you make an effort to educate others about what is going on inside your head. Often, another woman will have an easier time understanding your feelings than a man, simply because men are biologically inclined to think differently. Don't make it any harder on the men in your life to understand you by expecting them to know what is going on in your head. Start speaking your mind and getting your feelings out in a tactful way.

I have always had a hard time talking about my feelings, and let me tell you, I have a lot of big feelings! Ultimately, I believe this is better than not having any feelings at all, but it does make it *interesting* to deal with me. Half the time, I don't even know why I feel the way I do, which makes it challenging to try to explain it to someone else. But this is just what I need to do. The more you talk about it, the more you can get it out there.

Journaling can really help with getting any initial feelings out of the way so that the real meat of the issue can be addressed. Sometimes journaling, or writing in a diary, can help you think more logically. You need to realize that you cannot take your feelings out on others.

They are your feelings, and you are having those feelings because of something your mind is telling you. This also means you shouldn't take on other people's feelings. You are not responsible for other people's feelings and they are not responsible for yours. You cannot take their feelings personally and you need to know that they shouldn't take your feelings personally either.

That does not mean that you cannot be held responsible for your actions, or hold others responsible for their actions in life. If you do something in your life that causes an emotional reaction in someone, it is important to know what you did and how it made someone feel. Although you may not be responsible for that person's feelings, you do need to be held accountable for your actions.

The important thing to understand about all of this is that you need to be able to communicate your feelings, and why you are having them, in a rational and logical way. When you are feeling emotionally charged, especially in a negative way, it is generally not a great time to have a conversation with someone else. Better to hold off until you can calm yourself down. None of us want to say things that we don't mean just because we are hurt, angry, scared or jealous. So, when you are emotional, walk away from the situation for a few minutes, hours or days. Journal about your feelings and get your emotions out of the way. Scream, cry, hit a punching bag, go for a walk, lock yourself in the bathroom, or have a shower and, most importantly, breathe...

The whole point of having a conversation about your feelings is to get another person to understand why you are feeling a certain way and to communicate to them an understanding of why that feeling is there. Whatever that reason is, getting it out in the open will help you move forward in that relationship.

Communication is a two-way street. There is talking and listening and the goal should be an understanding, not necessarily a resolution of the problem. No one likes to be angry. The goal is to be happy. Happy people communicate their needs effectively, honestly and logically. Happy people listen effectively, honestly and logically. The results are impressive.

A big part of being an effective communicator is to be approachable. If you are smiling and making eye contact, other people will be drawn to you. Be aware of your body language. Standing with your arms folded in front of you tells people that you are "closed." Keep your hands out of your pockets, as this action suggests that you are uncomfortable or trying to hide something. If you need to do something with your hands, try holding them together loosely in front of you, which projects an air of professionalism.

When I am having a conversation with an individual or a group of people, I make a concerted effort to give them my undivided attention and try not to let other things distract me. When someone is looking around and losing focus when you are talking to them, you can tell they are not giving you their full attention. You can build a reputation as an amazing conversationalist by simply staying focused on the conversation you are having with someone. Train yourself to get in the conversation zone and you will almost forget that there is anything else going on around you. Trust me when I say that this will change the way people view you and it will absolutely change what you get out of your interactions with others. Just wait to see what you will learn and experience.

The Art Of Negotiation

Negotiating is just another form of communication. When you're negotiating with someone, never accept "no" as an answer. There is always something that can be done, even if they are telling you there isn't. So call them on it.

Be assertive about what you want — passionate even — and convey this to the person you are facing off against. Always negotiate so that both parties seem to "win." You need to convince them that what you are proposing will actually help them too. Listen carefully to the objectives or goals that the person you are dealing with has in mind. Listen to their objections and gather information. Ask lots of questions — you may have to ask them in different ways to get the right information. You need to be clever and bold enough to ask for what you want. And sometimes you have to be sweet and kind, even when you would rather scream.

BE THAT GIRL

Be accountable. Take responsibility for the things you do. If you say you are going to do something, do it!

When I am told: "There is nothing I can do for you," I always counter by saying: "Is there someone else that can help me then?" If someone else there has previously helped you do the same thing, or if another company has done it for you in the past, let the person you are dealing with know that you are aware that it is possible. Effective negotiators do whatever it takes. When you are buying anything, always ask if there is a sale, or a quantity discount, or any way the salesperson could give you better pricing. I love asking: "Is there a buy-today price deal?" when I'm negotiating with a salesperson, especially on a big-ticket item.

You never know how hungry the salesperson is to make that sale, and you just might hook yourself a good deal out of sheer timing. Asking these kinds of questions might make you feel nervous at first, but once you realize how often just asking for a better price can result in true savings, you will be asking every time and your positive results will increase accordingly.

When you are negotiating over money, the general rule is that whoever speaks first loses, so do your best to keep your money expectations to yourself until the other party has opened up the floor. The best example I can give of this is in a job interview.

If you are looking to secure a job position, you likely have an idea of how much you want to make in your head (and by now, you have completed your "Planet Do It Five Year Plan" so you know full well what your expectations are). Your potential employers will inevitably be asking you what your salary expectations are, but do not come right out and tell them.

Instead, dodge the subject a bit, saying something along the lines of: "Well, I'm just not sure what the industry standard is for this position right now. I know what I was making in my previous job, but before I come up with a figure for you I would like to know what you are looking to pay." Let *them* give *you* a number. Once they do (and they will start with the lowest amount they are willing to pay), you will have the upper hand. You have the power since you know what their lower limit is and they still do not know what your expectations are.

Don't ever undersell yourself. Ultimately, the more confident you are in the knowledge that you deserve to be paid well for what you do will encourage them to pay you more. Never settle just for what they give you. Always ask for more. You are worth it. Be confident in an interview setting and they will be begging you to come on board.

Where you sit, or stand, when you are involved in a negotiation (or any other situation for that matter) is extremely important. Always pick the power position if you are given the choice and do not be afraid to be the first one to select a seat. You need to be assertive and forward thinking to get what you want.

Always pick the seat with the best view of the entire room. Try not to sit with your back to the door, but instead choose the seat from which you have a clear view of the doorway or entrance. I have, on more than one occasion, been labeled a "control freak" when it comes to seating choice, but frankly my dears, I don't give a damn! I would rather have the upper hand and feel confident than worry about what people think.

Do not be afraid that others might perceive you as being "forward." This is not a bad thing. Most people want to be more assertive but are held back out of fear of being judged by others. Remember that this is your *life*. You are where you are because of you, and only you have the power to change that. So do not allow what others think control your actions. They are not living your life, you are. And you are going places… fast. Enjoy every moment of getting what you want. You don't have to be rude or aggressive, just forward and assertive.

At times, negotiating may make you feel that you are not being nice, but that's okay. It's important to be assertive, especially when you are managing others in a workplace setting, or trying to do what is right for you, your business or your family. Do not allow yourself to hold back on saying something important just because you think it might offend someone. Be convincing. If you prepare your arguments and plan to win, you will succeed.

The Need To Network

There's definitely truth to the saying: "It's all in who you know." Networking is very important, so make a concerted effort to associate with the right people.

Equally important is how you conduct yourself around important people. Don't be an "ass-kisser." People see right through that act.

Strive to network with people who inspire you and are doing things that you aspire to do in your life. Be honest and enthusiastic around those people. Be yourself, and always be on the lookout for opportunities. At the same time, you need to express your appreciation to those people in your life who deserve it: your boss, your coworkers and your staff, as well as your kids, your husband, your friends and your family. Be good to the people in your life and they will be good to you.

Don't be shy about leaving your business card everywhere

you go, with waiters and waitresses, store clerks, etc. You don't have to spend a lot of money to acquire business cards — in fact, some outlets, such as Vista Print, offer them for free. You never know when someone out there is going to need you or what you have to offer and vice versa. Brand and market yourself. Repeat the things that seem to work for you and let go of the things that don't get you the results you want.

If you have an idea, put it out there to as many people as you can. The more people that you can get to believe in your idea, and in you, the more powerful that idea will become. The more thoughts and energy that are being propelled towards your idea, the better chance you have of that idea coming to fruition. The power of positive thinking is amplified when the number of people who are thinking about a certain idea or project increases. I can attest to this: Be That Girl began as a small idea in my mind and look at it now!

When communicating with anyone in life make a point of treating them, and yourself, with respect. If you have respect for the person you are interacting with, you will be able to communicate more effectively.

Everyone has an opinion, and it may not necessarily be the same opinion as yours, but the most important part of communicating is to understand where the other person is coming from. This does not mean you have to agree with each other, just that you are able to have mutual respect for each other.

It can be tough sometimes not to judge someone based on their opinions about things, but in this case, it's good to remind yourself that we are all products of our environment and that it is our experiences that shape our beliefs. You cannot fault someone for that, but you can help them to see things in a different way. Be open minded and willing to listen and you never know what you can learn, or teach someone. Be patient enough to teach other people something that you think is valuable, and make an effort not to let strong emotions get in the way of expressing your opinions on things, especially in the workplace. It's better to come from a place of wit and logic rather than strong feelings.

All in all, never burn bridges. This is why it is so important to keep your emotions in check. We all know how it feels to lose touch with someone over a situation that gets out of hand. If that happens, let go, but then, in the future, try to do what you can to keep every contact in your Rolodex (or on an online site such as Facebook) at your fingertips. You never know when you are going to need those people.

CHAPTER 17

Don't Do It Alone

"Many hands make light work."
– John Heywood

Asking for help should not be looked at as a weakness. On the contrary, asking and accepting help is extremely powerful. When you help others, you are helping yourself. Teach others what you have learned, and you will learn it in a deeper and more meaningful way. In the end, you can't do it on your own. Well, technically you can, but there's a good chance the results will not be nearly as good.

Go Team!

I have a number of different teams in my life. My family is one of those teams (go team O'Connor!) We all work together toward common goals. Outside of my family, I have several other teams that I have assembled to work toward bringing my million-dollar ideas to fruition. With the formation of any team, the "rules of the game" and the goals and mission statements for that team need to be established clearly. Knowing this will help you decide which type of people you want on your team.

Ryan and I have been a solid team for years. Communication, teamwork, respect and a few pints of Guinness have kept our relationship strong and happy.

We are a team at O'Connor Acres. We love proving that it is more fun and productive when you do things together.

When the van needs detailing, Team O'Connor is there! My children know they are part of a team and they feel good participating in all of the activities that make a household run smoothly. You don't have to do it alone!

What values, morals and beliefs do the team members need to have? What will they get for being on the team? How will you decide who stays on the team and who doesn't? What are the expectations of each team member? If all of these things are defined up front, it will help you better assess potential candidates and it will make things less dicey when you are assessing performance. If there are performance standards up front, new team members will need to be informed of what those standards are. Having these guides in place goes a long way toward giving your team confidence and will give you a concrete way to assess team performance across the board.

Tell people when they do something great and let them know how much you appreciate them. Always focus on the positive characteristics of people, but do not sugarcoat things either when a difficult or sensitive issue requires attention. Bad apples are usually camouflaged. You need to use your gut when it comes to people and situations. If something (or someone) seems "too good to be true," then it usually is. Listen to that feeling in your gut and walk away when something seems just too good. Speak your mind tactfully. One of these days these boots are going to walk all over you? I don't think so!

Find a Coach

There is no way any of us can say we know how to do *everything*. All through our lives, learning opportunities are presented for the taking (or not). There is always someone out there waiting to teach you everything you need to know, at every point in your life, but you need to be watching, assessing and taking action to take advantage of this.

About 10 years ago, my mom met a "life coach" named Devlyn Steele. She was so excited about meeting him and about the program he was offering. My mom loves to share amazing things with her family, so she convinced me to try out Coach Steele's program, *Tools to Life*. I was skeptical, but I agreed to give it a shot.

My coaching consisted of a weekly phone call up to one hour combined with a weekly exercise/activity for a period of 90 days. After those 90 days, something in me had changed forever. I felt in control of my life and I had learned a lot about myself.

You need to allow yourself to be taught and in order for that to be possible you must be open and willing to experience things. You also need to be prepared to take responsibility for learning.

Having a coach in your life does not mean that they do things for you. Instead, they direct you to do things that will have an impact on your life. You do the work with their guidance. They may tell you what to do, but you are still the one responsible for taking action. A coach encourages you and helps you learn ways to take those actions. A coach helps you assess your performance, and encourages you to keep going.

My favorite part about having a "coach" is the accountability factor. If you are meeting with your coach on a weekly basis, be it on the phone or in person, and if you are given weekly tasks, you will feel accountable for those tasks, more so than if you were just doing those things of your own accord. If you have selected your coach or mentor carefully, they will be able to provide you with specific training so that you will learn what you need to know to succeed.

It is important to choose mentors who have done what you want to do. Mentors come in many forms. Anyone that helps you learn something positive can be seen as a mentor, or a coach. Your managers and bosses at work may be mentors to you. At the same time, you may have co-workers that you consider coach material as well. A mentor or coach need not be a personal acquaintance in your life. You may have mentors who are authors of inspiring and insightful books, and you may or may not ever meet them in person. They can still have a powerful influence on you.

The important thing here is to seek out insight from people who inspire you and who know more than you do about the things you might want to do with your life. Now that you know what you want in life, it is time to find the people out there who can help teach you what you need to know to get everything you want. Surround yourself with people who inspire you, and who create intense feelings of motivation inside you. Having a mentor in all areas of your life is essential for a successful and balanced lifestyle.

If you are a mom, you will need someone (or more than one person) to help you learn how to be a (better) parent at every different stage of your children's lives. There is no manual for new parents, so you need to seek out your own education in this area. There will be many different people offering you advice and training at each stage. Your education will come from books that you read and from people with whom you choose to surround yourself. The same thing goes for being a good companion, business owner, employee, friend or just being a better you.

Anytime you feel like you just do not know what to do next, with your kids, your business, yourself, or your life, you've got to ask for help. If things feel stagnant, and are not progressing as quickly as you would like, seek guidance. Ask for a mentor out loud and on paper. Write down what you need to learn and a mentor will show up to help you through it, if you want them, and if you are ready to jump on the opportunities as they arise.

Get Support

Life is not as good when you spend it all alone. We are social creatures and having other souls with similar needs and interests around us makes us feel comforted and happy. Having a partner in your life who is your best friend can enhance your life experience. Sharing your existence and energy with others is one of the joys that we humans are privy to in this life. Laughing, hugging, chatting, eating, feeling, playing and working are all more fulfilling when they are shared with others.

The more people that you have around you in your life, the less "work" life appears to be. When you have a large extended family and everyone agrees to bring one item to a dinner party, the dinner party is a snap for everyone involved. In the workplace, a project will always flow more smoothly, and happen faster, when you have a group of people all working together toward a common goal.

Similarly, if you and your family all work together as a team around your home with the cleaning and cooking and lunch-making, each person only needs to put a little effort in to see large results. Moms often feel overwhelmed with all of the tasks required of them in their homes. But it should not be all on mom to do everything! You and your partner and your kids are a team. The same thing goes for those people living with roommates. Every member of the household needs to contribute whatever they can to serve the greater good of the family or home unit. The next time you feel stressed about tasks in the home, don't hesitate to ask for more help from the other people living there.

Don't be shy about asking for help. No one expects you to do it all on your own. Speak up and remember that people cannot read your mind. Others may not realize what things they could be doing that would be helpful. Guide them by giving them tasks that they can do to contribute more to the team effort. Don't forget to be ridiculously positive and encouraging when you do get help. Tell the person helping you how much you appreciate it and you will be more likely to get help again in the future.

Now that you know how to get the help you need to accomplish anything, think about what it is you want to accomplish. Are you ready to start getting more results out of your life? Of course you are! It's time to talk shop.

"I read your book within a few days. The whole time thinking this sounds so great but come on like it is this easy. I kept thinking to myself I get the concept of like attracts like and the Universe providing, but doubted the entire possibility of it REALLY working. Three days later I went to the local goodwill and on the shelf in front of me were three books that I had wanted. Two of those books were books you had in Be That Girl...I guess the Universe heard me and also showed me that it COULD prove to ME that this is real and it does happen to people like me. So Cool!"

CHAPTER 18

Work It Girl!

"Choose a job you love, and you will never have to work a day in your life."
— Confucius

Thoughts produce actions. Actions produce results. What we want is results, but what we so often forget is that results require actions. We've got to work for those results.

Work. It's literally a four-letter word. Just hearing it can inflict panic in a lot of people, whether they realize it or not. Sunday night can be the most stressful night of the week as people are overcome with thoughts of getting up for work on Monday morning. Defined, as per the *Merriam-Webster Dictionary*, work is:

> Activity in which one exerts strength or faculties to do or perform something:
>
> **a :** sustained physical or mental effort to overcome obstacles and achieve an objective or result
>
> **b :** the labour, task, or duty that is one's accustomed means of livelihood

> **c :** a specific task, duty, function, or assignment often being a part or phase of some larger activity.

Work is perhaps best thought of as a simple exchange. We provide effort or time, and in exchange we are given something that has a perceived value.

On the other end of the spectrum, there is retirement. The concept of retirement evokes images of sunny, palm tree-lined beaches and serene lakefront cabins with wrap-around porches.

Reading books, traveling the world, skiing and golfing. Doing all the things you could be doing right now if it wasn't for work. Defined as per *Merriam-Webster*, retirement is:

> Withdrawal from one's position or occupation or from active working life.

The way we define retirement is in stopping the exchange of effort that was getting us the valued results. But do we want the results to stop? And are we really prepared to stop putting effort into our lives, just to be retired?

BE THAT GIRL

Long weekends are only long weekends if you have a job.

You hear so many stories of people who wait until they can "afford" to retire. At that point, they may be close to 65 years old. They completely stop putting in effort in their lives and have no plans to occupy their time or their minds. They get bored, lonely, unfulfilled, and poor and sooner, rather than later, they die. When it comes to this version of retirement, I say no thanks! I believe we need to change the way we think about work, and, by extension, retirement.

I feel like I "work" really hard. But I do not have a 9-to-5 job that I have to go to five days a week. I also do not have anyone telling me what I need to do everyday, or giving me deadlines for things. If I am unable to get things done during typical work hours (9 to 5), I come back to them once my children are in bed after 8 p.m. And if that is not enough, I will get up earlier to add some time to my day.

I need to stress that I have no one looking over my shoulder telling me what to do, or when to do it. I am my own boss, and I take full responsibility for the results that I see in my life as a result of my actions. I am in control of scheduling, prioritizing and ensuring that I get everything done, or that tasks are delegated to someone else to be completed on time.

I have full control of my time, and so do you. How you choose to spend your time will have a direct impact on the results you see in your life.

It's time for another exercise. Get out 2 fresh sheets of paper and your favorite pen. At the top of one sheet, write "My Efforts". Write out the following 4 headings, leaving several blank lines after each one.

1. **Personal**
    a.
    b.
    c.
2. **Family**
3. **Home**
4. **Monetary**

Now I want you to write down everything you do to fill your time in a given month. You should be able to categorize your efforts under one of the headings listed above.
Here is an example of "My Efforts" to get you going.

1. **Personal**
    a. Getting myself ready to face the day. (showering, hair, makeup, teeth-brushing, etc.).
    b. Having lunch each week with my mom and sister.
    c. Dates with my husband, at home or going out.
    d. Hanging out with my friends.
    e. Doing Yoga.
    f. Reading.
    g. Watching TV.

2. **Family**
    a. Getting my children ready for the day.
    b. Feeding my family breakfast and dinner.
    c. Making lunches for everyone to take to school, (done the day before to make mornings easier).
    d. Planning and scheduling the week for my family and myself.
    e. Driving my children to and from school, and organizing play dates with their friends.
    f. Doing homework with my children.
    g. Volunteering at school for each of my three children's classes.
    h. Grocery shopping.
    i. Organizing family functions, like brunches, birthday parties and dinners.

3. **Home**
    a. Making the beds everyday (currently, I make everyone's, although I am teaching my children the value of doing things for themselves as they get older).
    b. Tidying and cleaning the house.
    c. Laundry.
    d. Watering plants.

4. **Monetary**
    a. Running On the Rocks liquor stores.

b. Generating the e-newsletter for the liquor stores.
c. Writing and Posting Be That Girl's "Inspirations".
d. Writing books.
e. Communicating with lawyers and accountants about issues related to our businesses.
f. Doing online research for business opportunities.
g. Doing book signings.
h. Participating in conference calls for the industry board that I am involved in, and attending out-of-town meetings for this board.
i. Hauling cases of beer, wine and spirits when they arrive at our stores on order days (my workout!).
j. Working on my websites.

It is truly amazing to consider what you do with the time you have. Just looking over this list will give you a new perspective on your time.

Now it's time to assess your results. On the second piece of paper, write "My Results" at the top of the page. Write the same 4 headings that you used on your efforts page, making sure you leave several blank spaces between each one.

1. **Personal**
    a.
    b.
    c.
2. **Family**
3. **Home**
4. **Monetary**

For each line item on your efforts page, I want you to consider what result(s) you are getting, and then write them down. Do not be concerned if each effort does not have its own result. Some efforts combine to produce one result.

Here is an example of "My Results".

1. **Personal**
    a. I get noticed!
    b. I am in good physical shape.
    c. I have strong, close bonds with my family and friends.
    d. I am prepared, organized and (mostly) calm.

2. **Family**
    a. I have happy, healthy children who get what they need in terms of love, attention, food, clothing, etc.
    b. Our family is not rushed in the morning. We all have a hearty breakfast together and everyone gets out of the house on time, feeling ready to take on the day. Everyone leaves the house with a prepared lunch. This saves time and money, and ensures that everyone eats something healthy.

3. **Home**
    a. I feel relaxed about the state of my home. Having things neat and tidy gives me a sense of order and allows me to focus on the tasks of the day.
    b. We all have clean clothes!
    c. My plants create cleaner air and positive energy.

4. **Monetary**
    a. The liquor store businesses are successful, giving me the lifestyle freedom that I want with the rewards of owning a business. (You may choose to write down how much money you receive in exchange for your efforts).
    b. I am learning everyday how to be better at everything.
    c. I inspire people (including myself) everyday.
    d. I generate enough money to suit the lifestyle that I want, and I have plans to make enough money to help others have better lifestyles too.

Now look over both of your lists, and answer the following questions. Ponder the questions in your own mind, and then write down your answers in your journal. You know now how powerful writing things down can be!

- How do you feel about how you are spending your time?
- Are you balancing your time well across all categories, or is your time being focused largely on one category?
- Are you getting the results you want in each category? Is there room for improvement?
- Do you feel that the exchange you make in time is worth what you are receiving? Do you feel like you are giving up more than you are receiving?

We are all our own bosses in life. We are in charge of the results that we see. We are the only ones that can be held responsible for where we are and this gives us the ultimate power over where we are going in our lives.

If you are not happy with the current results, you have two choices:

1. **Do something different.**
2. **Change the way you think.**

No matter what you decide to do, you must be prepared to put in the effort and take action in your life. You must do the work, put in the time, learn more and strive for more.

Changing what you do can be simple or hard. It can be something small, or something big. It can be exciting, or it can be stressful. Often the difference is a matter of your own perception. Get excited about change, as it is the only thing in this life that is inevitable. Standing still and taking no action will end in little or no positive results. Always take action.

Remember that being busy does not equal being successful. You do not need to justify your existence by being busy all the time. A big part of being That Girl is learning to distinguish between being successful and being a control freak.

Don't let yourself get bored. Instead, be stimulated by books, hobbies, further education, cooking classes or learning new languages. If your current work is not your passion, change it! I was recently in a Hallmark store and saw a card that said: "Follow your passion, not your pension." Nothing could be more true!

Now, how can you make things better in your life? Remember that you only have two options; create tangible change in your life, or create change in your thoughts.

If you have decided to change something in your life, you must also give yourself the power to feel excited about this change. You know that you want to change something. You have decided to proceed. You have taken the biggest step to success. You've made a decision, now stick to it.

Be accountable to yourself. Get excited about your own power. Take the control back. And never, ever, let fear stand in the way of your dreams again.

You have huge dreams of amazing results in your life. You cannot get to those results unless you stay focused and start taking action to achieve those goals, and that means change. Get into the groove of embracing change. Once you convince yourself to embrace change, you will find yourself more excited about what each day will bring.

If you decide not to change what you are doing, you have only one other choice and that is to change your thinking. Stop complaining about being unhappy with the results in your life. You have the power to change those results and you have chosen not to, so you must actually be happy with what you have. Imagine that! "*You got to ac-cent-tchu-ate the positive and e-lim-i-nate the negative...*" Harold Arlen and Johnny Mercer sure knew what they were talking about.

Instead of complaining and feeling unhappy about things, do this instead: every morning when you wake up, think of one amazing thing about your life and write it down. You should still have your journal on the go, so just use that. No need to date anything or write any more than a sentence.

Think of something new every day. Balance your thinking to include amazing things from all the different areas of your life as the weeks progress:

- **Relationships**
  My husband remembered what I wanted for my birthday and got it for me... all by himself!

- **Efforts (Work, School, Volunteering)**
  My boss lets me take an extra long lunch on Fridays and pays for my cellphone.

- **Home**
  Our roof is no longer leaking.

- **Results (Paycheck, Free Time, Vacation, Things)**
  I volunteer at my children's school and take three weeks of vacation every year without hassle.

- **Health**
  I haven't come down with a cold all winter long.

- **Self**
  I sat and had a coffee by myself today and read my book for one hour.

Try to do this everyday, and keep it going forever. Even when things get you down, there is always one thing in your life that is positive. Remember the positive things and focus on them. The human mind can only hold one thought at a time, make it a good one.

Do not worry or complain. You will create whatever you think about in your life, so what have you been creating lately? Are you satisfied? Start creating new results if you're not. It's simple. Two choices. Door number one: do something different or door number two: change the way you think. And remember, you are in control. Take the reins and let happiness start pouring into your life everyday. It's all in your perspective and your actions.

If you want to continue taking action until you are over 100, you will need to keep yourself in good health. Read on for some simple, everyday strategies to keep you healthy, vibrant and energetic.

Chapter 19

Be Well

"When the breath wanders the mind also is unsteady. But when the breath is calmed the mind too will be still, and the yogi achieves long life. Therefore, one should learn to control the breath."
– Hatha Yoga Pradipika

After I completed my degree in Psychology, I realized that I wasn't so passionate about my chosen field of study. I really wanted to help people — I certainly was passionate about that — but I found psychology, as a discipline, to be somewhat nebulous and subjective. I am a concrete person. I like there to be a logical answer for everything. However, an example of what I learned in Psychology is that when diagnosing depression, the patient is evaluated based on a list of symptoms, and basically, anyone who exhibits a certain number of the symptoms could be considered depressed. But even if that patient has all of the listed symptoms, it does not mean they *are* depressed, since the diagnosis is based on how adversely the patient's life is being affected than on the exact symptoms. I found myself considering that if the process of diagnosis was that abstract, and if the methods of actually treating mental illness were so ambiguous, then I had very little control over the situation.

I felt increasingly frustrated by the idea that there were no concrete answers to mental illness, which inspired me to redirect my energy into the field of neuroscience, where the studies seemed more tangible and objective. But hanging out with rats in the dungeon of the university by myself was not doing it for me either and eventually I made the decision to move on. In a sense, the drive to help people that began with my interest in psychology has led to the creation of this book. I see Be That Girl as an outlet for me to help people — as many people as I possibly can.

Now, don't get me wrong. I still have a great respect for the field of psychology and the gains it has made in treating and helping people. My decision not to pursue it was personal and specific to my own philosophies. I do feel that we have to be responsible and aware of our own health, which includes mental and physical health. Being healthy is a key part of being That Girl.

On that note, here are some tips to help you be well while you are out there being amazing.

BE THAT GIRL

There is a natural way to fight off the flu. You don't need to get that nasty shot that might make you sick. Build up your immune system instead.

Homeopathy And The Natural Medicine Cabinet

When I was pregnant with my second daughter, I opted for a midwife instead of going through my regular doctor. My midwife introduced me to several natural remedies to use while I was pregnant and directly after the birth. There are a lot of natural things you can take or do that will help your body heal itself. I am not totally against what we would call "traditional medicine," and

I still use the medical system on an "as need" basis, but I like to try to do things more naturally first. For example, antibiotics are great for killing the bad germs in your body, but antibiotics also kill the good germs in your body. Probiotics replace the good, healthy bacteria in your body. When you take antibiotics without probiotics, you may end up with an imbalance of bacteria in your body, which can result in a yeast infection. In addition to that, your body builds up immunity to the antibiotics very quickly, making future treatments less effective, or not effective at all.

When my oldest daughter was about two years old, she got an ear infection. The doctor put her on antibiotics, which seemed to do the trick at first. But the ear infection eventually flared up again two more times. After several more rounds of antibiotics without any success, I decided there had to be something else I could do. A couple of my friends were into "natural medicine" and they recommended I go that route. I proceeded to a local health food store and was introduced to something called colloidal silver — basically water with silver ions in it. Even though it sounds simple, colloidal silver is a natural antibiotic that has multiple uses. I followed the instructions given to me by the staff and put some drops into my daughter's ear. I also gave her the silver orally. Within several hours she was feeling much better. Within two days, her ear infection was gone and it has not come back since.

Now, in the event any of my three daughters complain of sore ears, I immediately treat them with drops of colloidal silver and I never hear another word about it. The quicker you can get on top of any health condition, the easier it will be to control it. Being aware of your body and having confidence in using natural remedies can keep you healthy for years to come.

After my first introduction to natural medicine I was hooked and needed to learn more. My advice is to find a natural or whole food store close to your home and then go in and ask lots of questions. My initial frustration with these places was that they assumed I already had a base of knowledge. They assumed I knew how to take homeopathic remedies properly, or that I already knew about the other uses of colloidal silver (maybe I was taking the fake it 'til you make it concept a little far!). But I hung in there and asked the questions I needed to ask and eventually got the information I needed.

Do not be afraid to admit that you do not know things. It is far better to ask for more information instead of doing things incorrectly. Be an information seeker, and always ask for clarification if you don't quite get it. Learn by asking! And make sure you understand the directions, especially when it comes to your health.

Now, anytime there is a health-related issue in our family, I go straight to my homeopath. There is rarely a lineup and I don't waste time waiting around in a room with a bunch of sick people (as I would at a walk-in clinic). I explain my situation, and they ask me a series of questions to determine which remedy will work best. I get my little sugar pills, take a dose (or give a dose) right away and I go home.

If I cannot cure something naturally, I will still proceed to the doctor — I am not so stubborn to refuse to take something just because it is not natural. I still have Tylenol and Ibuprofen in my medicine cabinet but I always think twice now before gulping it down, pausing first to consider whether or not there might be something natural that I could take instead. Thinking along those lines, here are the essential, everyday items to have in your natural-medicine cabinet:

- **Colloidal Or Ionic Silver**
  (either or, depending on what's available)
  Usually sold as a liquid in a few different sizes, I would recommend buying a larger bottle as it has a lot of uses. You will also want to buy a "silver accessory kit," consisting of three glass bottles, one with a press-spray lid, one with a dropper and one that looks like a nasal sprayer. Use glass containers whenever possible and not clear

bottles, as light can affect your remedies. Pour some of your silver into each bottle so that you can use it appropriately (you may need to drop some into an eye or ear, or spray some of it onto a cut or into the back of your throat. Never use a metal spoon, or any other metal when you are dosing with silver, as the metal will counteract with the silver and it won't work. I use small medicine cups, or a plastic measuring spoon. Silver is a natural antibiotic so it can be used for almost anything. Before you run to traditional medicines, always consider the option of using silver first. Here are just a few common uses:

- Eye, ear or nose infections: take orally and dose directly into the orifice.
- Colds and flu: take orally. In the case of a sore throat, spray the back of the throat a few times as well.
- Cuts, sunburns and rashes: use to stimulate healing. Also effective on insect bites – spray silver directly on the affected area.
- Acne: apply topically.
- Wart removal and nail-fungus treatment. Spray onto affected area twice daily.
- Kitchen disinfectant: works as a germ-killer on cutting boards and counter surfaces. Can also be used on phones and keyboards as an antibacterial agent.
- Purification: add a few drops to water if you are unsure of its purity.

- **Arnica Gel and Arnica Pellets**

  For muscle pain, bumps and bruises. Take the pellets orally or apply the gel right to the affected area. Arnica promotes healing of damaged tissue. I took it immediately following childbirth and I was amazed at how fast and effective it was at relieving my pain. It is not to be used on open wounds, so, if you have a cut, use something else, like silver or calendula.

My natural medicine cabinet. My homeopathic pellet tubes are held together with an elastic, shown on the far left. The Arnica gel is behind the pellets. Directly in the center is my bottle of Silver, along with 2 of the accessory bottles, the dropper and the sprayer. The allergy pills are in the box to the right of the silver, and the oil of oregano is on the far right. I pack all of this stuff with me when I travel anywhere. Go natural!

- **Calendula Gel and Tincture**
  For cuts, scrapes and skin irritations like sunburn. Use this instead of antibiotic ointment. The tincture is a liquid form of calendula that can be mixed with water and used as a rinse to promote healing to the skin. There are some hand creams on the market that have calendula in them and are great for healing dry, cracked skin. It is a very soothing gel.

- **Pascallerg Allergy Pills**
  Improper dosing of mainstream allergy and cold medications has caused deaths in children, so I am reluctant to give them to my family. Pascallerg is a natural allergy pill that doesn't cause drowsiness or have any other adverse side affects. They are awesome for kids – my daughter Kayley has multiple allergies and chews them like candy. They work like a charm for anyone with allergies.

- **Oil of Oregano**

  This stuff tastes awful, but it sure is effective in killing germs! Use it for skin conditions, digestive problems, sinus congestion and to ward off an oncoming cold or flu. (Personally, I start with silver, and if that is not effective, I'll try this).

  Do not take Oil of Oregano if you are pregnant.

So those are the main items you need in your natural medicine cabinet. Everything else can be obtained on an as-need basis.

A Note on Fever

When you have a fever, your body is heating itself up in order to fight off and destroy whatever foreign invaders are in there.

Having a fever is actually a healthy, normal defense mechanism that your body uses to protect itself. If you immediately reach for the Tylenol or Ibuprofen to reduce the fever, you will actually be inhibiting the body's ability to do its job. Even if you have a febrile seizure from a fever, it is not anything to worry about. Do not put yourself or anyone else in a cold bath with a fever, you're better off to let the fever run its course.

Thinking along the same lines, if you are not feeling well and you are fighting a virus, simulate a fever. Wrap yourself up in lots of clothes and burrow under loads of blankets. This will create a heat within your body that will sizzle up the germs. A hot bath (really hot!) or shower will also help to increase the body temperature. Use what you have been given.

Drink Water

We have all heard this a million times before, but that's because it's super important. Personally, I do not like cold water or cold drinks, so I mostly get my fluids through drinking tea. I drink a combination of caffeinated tea, herbal tea, and straight hot water throughout the day. The warmness makes me feel so good and warm drinks are said to be better for your body as your bodily fluids are similarly warm.

Just as hot drinks are relaxing, cold drinks are stimulating. Introducing freezing cold water into your body can be a shock to your system and your body will burn calories to heat up this cold water. While this calorie burning may seem like a good idea if you're trying to shed a few pounds, it can also be considered as wasted energy and time.

Hot drinks stimulate digestion, while cold water with a meal may slow down digestion. Hot water is ready for the body to use and it helps break the food down faster.

Cold water can solidify fats rather than breaking them down, making it harder for the body to purge that fat. If you want to make a simple change that will help you maintain a healthier lifestyle, drink more hot water. Start with room temperature water if you need to. As an added bonus, boiled water is likely cleaner than cold water as some of the impurities are removed through the boiling process.

Be Active

The key to leading an active lifestyle is doing things that you enjoy. If you love to golf, do more of it. Love softball, baseball, soccer, hockey or volleyball? Find a community team that you can join and get out and be active at least once a week. If you hate going to the gym, but bought a membership because you knew if you bought a membership you would guilt yourself into going, you are setting yourself up to fail. To ensure success, all you have to do is change your thinking about the gym. Start telling yourself how much you enjoy going to the gym. Maybe you love the steam room afterwards or you love looking at all the hot guys (or girls) while you are working out. Maybe you love the way your muscles feel after a grueling workout. See, it's not so hard to be positive about the gym after all!

Another way to be active is to opt for a job that involves some activity. I love working at my liquor stores on the day the order is delivered, helping out with hauling the heavy boxes of wine, spirits and beer. It keeps my muscles tight and I even get in some cardio from all the walking back and forth as we bring the cases into the stores. Ask yourself if there's a way for you to be more active in your job, or find a new one that allows you to move around.

Optimize Your Weight

My mom says the secret to staying slim is to eat less and move more. I say it is to eat enough of the right foods and exercise enough to maintain a good metabolism. If you are aiming to lose weight, start thinking like a slender girl.

Start imagining you already have the body you've always wanted. How will you look in the mirror? What kind of clothes will you wear? How will you feel in that body? How will others treat you when you have reached your ideal weight goal?

Once you have an idea of what you'll look like, start thinking like That Girl, living the life she would lead, and do it now (fake it 'til you make it!). You can achieve anything that you put your mind to, so start putting it into the fit-girl mindset. Realize that you have full control over how you look. Start seeing yourself as that slender person and you will subconsciously make the right choices in your life to get there.

Eat Well

Eat breakfast within one hour of waking up. Your body has essentially starved through the night and if you do not feed it first thing in the morning it will begin to conserve fat. The body is smart enough to save itself. If it thinks it is starving, it will hang on to fat for dear life.

Feed yourself often. Eat small portions frequently throughout the day. I keep a lunch bag (my sister calls it the "feedbag") with me at all times, as well as a stash of emergency items in the car (granola bars and other items that hold up well). Focus on eating lots of fruits and vegetables, the greener and leafier, the better. More green and leafy equals more nutrients. I also like to eat eggs. One hardboiled egg gives you a ton of energy and some decent fats, plus it is simple to prepare. You can boil a few at a time and they will keep in the fridge for a few days. As long as you are active, a hardboiled egg makes a great snack.

Probiotic yogurt with flax seed is another super-food. Flax is the new miracle grain. Flax seed can actually increase your estrogen levels, which can help minimize negative menopause symptoms and may also help prevent some diseases. All women should be eating flax regularly; about a tablespoon a day. It's best to buy it whole (pre-ground flax goes rancid easily) and it should be kept in an airtight container. Before eating the flax seed, grind it in a coffee grinder. Your body will not be able to digest it whole. Grind a few days' worth and store the ground seeds in the fridge for up to a week.

Eat Simple

Limit your intake of processed food as much as you can. The closer the food is to its natural state, the better for you it will be. When you are grocery shopping, try not to venture into the middle aisles. This is where you will find most of the processed items. Keep it simple and basic. Steam your vegetables or eat them raw. Steaming keeps the vitamins inside the vegetables instead of draining them away down the sink with the water used to boil them. Eat real butter. Do not substitute margarine. You're better off sticking to the natural goodness of butter, but just using less. Stay away from fancy sauces and dressings. They add flavor, but they also add an abundance of calories and fat. And what is in those sauces anyway? If you cannot pronounce it, don't eat it. Instead, use spices to season your food or make salsa your sauce of choice. Salsa is a great way to add flavor and vegetables to your diet without adding a lot of fat, plus, it's easy to make fresh.

Change Your Thinking

Slender girls love salads and they enjoy preparing and cutting all those vegetables. If you think it is hard to prepare healthy snacks and meals, think about how it would have been back in the day when you had to grow your own food first. Don't be lazy or whiny. Cut up those vegetables and enjoy doing it. Eliminate anything deep-fried from your diet.

At restaurants, share a meal with someone instead of ordering your own — portion size is crucial for maintaining a healthy weight. Anytime you have dessert, have a small portion. Remember: everything in moderation. This includes food, alcohol and everything else. Balance your life. If you are eating appropriately, I do not believe you need to add vitamin supplements to your diet. Vitamins have always made me feel sick to my stomach. Too much of anything all at once is never a good thing.

Take Resveratrol

You might have heard about the health benefits of red wine, however, drinking too many glasses of wine is not ideal because of the alcohol content. Resveratrol is an anti-aging compound derived from red-wine grapes that appears to actually repair cells. A resveratrol supplement allows you to reap the benefits of a high-concentration of red-wine grapes without all the alcohol ingestion. There are several brands of resveratrol supplements on the market — the Shaklee line of products makes a great one called Vivex and the Sisel line of products has one called Eternity. The liquid form is the most concentrated and easiest to digest.

Practice Yoga

Yoga is one of the most invigorating activities you can do, but it is also gentle on the body. Yoga is a very personal activity, one that invites each person to do only what they can, with a focus on personal goals. It keeps you flexible, helps with chronic pain issues and it will make your body feel terrific. Yoga is also amazing for the mind. If you want to reconnect yourself to the Universe, start practicing yoga.

Yoga can also tone you in ways that you never thought possible. Doing yoga can help you achieve all of your physical goals and it can increase your quality of life both now and as you age. Seeing 80-year-olds kick my butt at yoga is extremely motivating. I am determined to be one of those yoga-goddess grannies!

Get your *Zzzzzz's*

Sleep is essential, so make it a priority to get your zzzz's. Decide when you need to get up in the morning so you won't feel rushed and make sure you go to bed early enough to make that happen. Make the effort to get up in enough time to be prepared for your day. You need time to get yourself ready, eat breakfast, get your family ready, exercise and maybe get a bit of work done. What time do you have to get up to get all those things done and still be out of the house on time? That's the time you need to get up. Don't compromise. Kick your own butt out of bed in the morning and be excited about your day. Based on the time you need to wake up in the morning, revise your bedtime so you are getting seven-to-eight hours of sleep every night. If you want to get up at 5 a.m., get to bed by 10 p.m. That is, in bed, asleep by 10 p.m., so you'll need to plan to start your bedtime routine at 9:30 p.m.

Quit Smoking

I started smoking when I was 13 years old. Looking back, I wish I had listened to my parents when they told me not to smoke. Ryan and I were both smokers and when we were ready to quit we tried everything: the patch, Zyban (an antidepressant that is believed to help people quit smoking), acupressure and acupuncture, fake cigarettes, cold turkey... nothing seemed to work! Finally, we were introduced to a book called *Easyway to Stop Smoking* by Allen Carr (theeasywaytostopsmoking.com). This book deals with the psychology of smoking. Yes, smoking is physically addictive, but if you change your thinking about smoking, your chances of successfully quitting will improve significantly.

I highly recommend Carr's method, so check it out if you're struggling with quitting too. You know smoking is bad for you, and you know you want to quit, so do it now.

Take a Time Out

If you are not feeling well, do not keep soldiering on. Give yourself a rest period when you are feeling ill and your body will be better able to heal itself. Trust me when I say that I know there is never an ideal time to take a rest period, but you have to force it on yourself — taking one day off may prevent you needing to take a week off at a later date because you got even sicker. Do not feel guilty about getting rest as soon as your body needs it. Resting your body conserves energy, allowing your body to use that extra energy to fight off whatever is afflicting you. Help your body out by taking the rest as soon as you feel something coming on.

Shit, Or Get Off The Pot

A sure sign that your body is functioning well is if you are having regular and healthy bowel movements (BMs). The waste products created by food need to get out of your body as quickly as possible — having waste sitting in your intestines for a long period of time is not good. The water, fruits and fibre you consume all work to keep things moving. The optimum frequency for BM's varies widely. Some people have a BM after every meal, some once a day and some people every couple of days. Everyone is different in this area, but my advice would be to strive for once a day.

You will know you are eating properly when you have regular BMs. When you eat too much cheese, red wine and baguettes, you will notice a major difference in your regularity. Also, your BMs should be easy to manage. You should not have to sit on the toilet for 20 minutes. Having a BM should not be the perfect time to catch up on your book or magazine! You should not have to expend much effort, either. In fact, too much squeezing and sitting on the john can cause hemorrhoids and other health issues.

Taking probiotic supplements can be helpful in this area. Probiotics are essentially good bacteria that can help with digestion. Probiotic pills (which can be found at any natural or health food store), combined with a proper diet, will have you feeling good and regular in no time.

Judge your health by your BMs and if you are not satisfied with what you see and smell (or how you feel), take action now!

Don't Hold Back

Never hold your urine or your BM longer than is necessary. When you feel the urge to go, try to go right away. Holding in your urine for extended periods can stretch out your bladder, which can lead to incontinence later in life. And holding in BMs can cause constipation. If you have issues using public toilets, you need to change your thinking. The health issues that can result from holding it in are not worth it. Why would you want your waste products to stay in your body any longer than they have to, anyway?

You can easily change your health habits just by applying a few simple strategies and by changing how you think about your health and your body. Treat your body well, and it will treat you well for years to come. Enjoy being a healthier you starting today.

Epilogue

"Your present circumstances don't determine where you can go; they merely determine where you start."
— Nido Qubein

I want to thank you for spending your time with me. I am so excited to see what you will do with the information that you have been given.

If you have taken my advice seriously, you will have already started making some small changes in your life. If you have taken action, you will already be seeing results, even if they are small. All those results are going to add up… quickly.

I like the saying "the proof is in the pudding." It basically means that you should take seriously the results that you see around you, and use those as a basis upon which to make decisions. Results do not lie. Take advice, education and training only from those who are actually getting the desired results.

Have you ever had someone tell you: "Do as I say, not as I do?" That's not the case here. I want you to do as I do, and do as others before me have done. Come into my house anytime and you'll see that I am practicing everything I preach. If you want to see the results of my actions, just check out my life. I'm the real deal! And so are you.

I honestly believe that if you apply even just one of the principles laid out in Be That Girl, you *will* see positive changes in your life. There will be certain parts of the book that will inspire you to take action now and you should focus on those parts to start. As you start to change things, and get more and more results, you will inevitably start changing more things and continue getting bigger results…

I trust that you are starting to feel an extreme confidence in yourself and in your abilities. You must believe that you can do anything. That is the way to make it all happen.

You are at the helm of your own adventure. You can chart your own path. You are in control. You are in the driver's seat. Knowing this intuitively — really knowing it — is the key to the infinite Universe, and all of the possibilities it has for you.

See your success. Envision it always and know what it looks like and feels like. Write it down. Take action. Assess opportunities and jump on the right ones. Ask for help. Have Faith. Smile. And be thankful.

Now go and be wildly successful. And keep in touch!

Tina

Acknowledgements

"Lots of people want to ride with you in the limo, but what you want is someone who will take the bus with you when the limo breaks down."
– Oprah Winfrey

I would like to take this opportunity to say that I did not get here alone. I may talk tough and I am certainly an independent soul, but I love and need amazing people surrounding me and supporting me. I am That Girl because of the people in my life. Thank you to all of you who are sharing this journey with me. With you, I am more.

Ryan O'Connor, you are the light in my life and the love in my heart. I knew the moment I first met you that there was something drawing us together. It was no coincidence that we met and that we are so perfectly paired. You have always believed in me, been supportive of me, and been forgiving of me. You bring out the best in me, but you also don't put up with my crap. You help me to slow down and think just a little, while still encouraging me when I decide to leap forward without much thought. You are the yin to my yang and the tiger to my dragon.

To my beautiful daughters, Trinity, Kayley and Payton: Sorry that I have been ignoring you and letting you watch too much TV while I have been scrambling to finish this book. But you are wonderful, independent girls and I know you can handle it. Go Team O'Connor!

To my mom, Janet Legere, online guru extraordinaire. Thank you so much for nurturing my independence (even if you didn't want to at times) and for teaching me how to build my own website, and put on a webinar. And thank you for all your "grand-parenting" (babysitting).

Oh, Lil' Shelley (a.k.a. Shelley Arnusch). From our first meeting about Be That Girl, I knew it was going to be an exciting ride with you on board. You have done an amazing job of editing this book. Thank you for sharing my excitement and trusting in me. You are witty, smart, and trés chic and your karaoke skills and tickle trunk are enviable. Together, we planned it and did it, girl! You ROCK!

Ashleigh Fryklind, you jumped at the chance to work on this project and your enthusiasm hasn't faded! You have successfully kept me on track with deadlines, you believed in me, and you have kept me motivated. You are not afraid to take on any task and you know where to look to find what you need when you need it. I am blessed to have you on my team.

Misty Brownlee, my partner in crime. You have been the "rock" in On the Rocks ever since you came on board. Your calm intensity, leadership and ability to take on the world everyday is inspiring, and it sets my mind at ease. You just know how to handle things. Thank you for your help with the Be That Girl presentation, we finished it just in time! And hey, one quick run through is all you need when you have an amazing team in place! Fake it 'til you make it worked again! I am looking forward to sharing more *interesting* moments with you.

To my amazing book designer, Tania Craan. You have been patient and understanding with me through the book design process, and you never laughed (out loud) at my crazy insecurities about other people's opinions. You have provided me with incredible advice and direction beyond book design, and you have been a source of incredible calmness. I look forward to our next adventure together!

To my incredible mentors (you know who you are!), my success is a direct reflection of the guidance, knowledge and experience that you have imparted onto me. My success is proof positive that networking with those who have already done what you want to do can fast track your own projects. Instead of letting me learn the hard way, you have walked me down a path paved with only smooth stones. I feel blessed that you committed time out of your own busy lives to help me. Good Karma is on its way to you, my treasured mentors!

To my very best friend in the whole wide world, Annie. You and I are stuck together like glue. You have been supplying me with books for years now and your selections always seem to be just what I need, when I need it. I am looking forward to growing old with you as my buddy.

Inspiration and support have been around me all my life. I have chosen to embrace it, and I have been rewarded with all of you. *Namaste.*